Accessing Guic

Accessing Clear Guidance

Help and Answers Through
Inspired Writing and Inner Knowing

Accessing Guidance Series

Accessing Guidance: Intuitive Linked Communication (ILC), Volume 1 by Frank DeMarco

Accessing Clear Guidance: Help and Answers Through Inspired Writing and Inner Knowing, Volume 2 by Ruth Shilling

Books and Cards by Ruth Shilling

Through A Medium's Eyes Series: About Life, Love, Mediumship, and the Spirit World
- Rev. B. Anne Gehman, Volume 1 (also in LARGE PRINT)
- Carol Gasber, Volume 2
- Neal Rzepkowski, M.D., Volume 3

Violin Success Series
- Success with the Violin & Life: Strategies, Techniques, and Tips for Learning Quickly and Doing Well, Volume 1
- Performing at Your Best: A Musician's Guide to Successful Performances, Volume 2

The Tomb of Queen Nefertari: Egyptian Gods and Goddesses of the New Kingdom

Time & Space in the Temples & Pyramids: All One World Egypt Tour

SINAI: The Desert & Bedouins of South Sinai's Central Regions (photo book)

Ancient Egyptian Gods & Goddess Cards

"Color It True" Manifestation Mandalas Coloring Book Series,
- Marvelous Manifestation Mandalas, Volume 1
- Magnetic Manifestation Mandalas, Volume 2
- Miraculous Manifestation Mandalas, Volume 3
- Angelic Manifestation Mandalas, Volume 4

Accessing Guidance Series – No. 2

Accessing Clear Guidance

Help and Answers Through Inspired Writing and Inner Knowing

RUTH SHILLING

All One World Books & Media

Print book ISBN: 978-1-945963-44-5
eBook ISBN: 978-1-945963-45-2

Published by All One World Books & Media,
Rhode Island, USA, all1world.com

Text, interior illustrations, and cover design:
Ruth Shilling, ruthshilling.com

Table of Contents

Introduction

Is it possible to know what to do even if you are in a brand-new situation, something you have never experienced before?

This is the question that came up for me after I heard the following story. I do not know if this whole story is actually true (although parts of it certainly are), but that is not the point here. What matters is that this story got me thinking about the possibility that there is a way to know the right thing to do even if it is something we have never encountered before.

Here's the story.

In December of 1984 in Bhopal, India, there was a terrible disaster. A Union Carbide chemical plant began spewing out toxic gas. It poured out into the surrounding villages killing more than 2,000 people.

Everyone panicked. There was chaos as people screamed, "RUN! RUN! RUN!" The streets were filled with people running to get away from it.

But in one of the villages, there was a woman who did not run. Her belief was, "When in doubt, meditate." So, instead of running, she sat in meditation and calmed herself. Then she asked, "What should I do?"

The answer came, "Turn on the fan. Lie down, and go to sleep." So that is what she did.

She was the only person in that village to survive. The people who were running in the streets were gulping the toxic fumes into their lungs and soon died. As the woman lay in the house, her breathing was shallow and slow. Somehow the fan moving the air also helped.

As I said, I don't know if this story is really true, but it introduced me to the idea that help is available if we learn to listen for it. The information about the way to survive the chemical disaster was there and available to every person in the village. However, this one woman was the only one who asked for that information, listened, and followed it.

This focused me on a quest to learn more and to find out if it was indeed a real possibility, and if so, to see if I could develop that skill myself.

Now, decades later, having successfully developed it, I want to share it with you.

Developing Intuition and Inner Knowing

I worked on this through two basic avenues, 1) getting wise guidance through journaling and 2) doing different experiments to discern the intuitive feelings that could point me in the right directions as I went about my day.

You will find here lots of useful information about how it can work for you, but it is by doing the hands-on experiments that you will develop the skills yourself. Getting all these benefits in your own daily life is what really matters!

So let's get started.

I would be delighted to hear about your successes with this. If you email me about them (a1w.books@gmail.com), we can celebrate together. What benefits one of us, benefits the whole!

CHAPTER ONE

Everyday Choices

How Can You Know
What Will Be Best?

Should I take that job? Buy that house? Is this the man I should marry? How can I gracefully get out of this marriage? Is this a good time to start a new business? Can I trust this person? What should I make for dinner? Is it worth buying that book? Should I turn left or right?

Every day of our lives is full of decisions, choices about all kinds of things – from the clothes we put on in the morning, products we buy, what task we do first, and commitments we make. It is an endless stream of "this or that?"

Sometimes those choices are easy. We have definite options and we can see which ones are beneficial. But what about the ones where the information that would make choosing easy is not available? How can you possibly know if your life would be better if you choose one university over another? You can weigh up the information you have, but in the end, you will never *really* know.

Thank Goodness I Listened!

On Monday, March 9, 2020, I was in Cairo Egypt. Having just completed hosting two 15-day tours of Egypt, I was ready to kick back and relax for a week at a friend's house. I was especially looking forward to playing with the kids and being free of all the responsibilities that came with being in charge of a tour group.

I had been so busy that I had not spent any time online, so once I was all settled and cozy in their guestroom, I booted up my laptop and went online. I saw that the new COVID-19 virus was getting some headlines, but I didn't feel any urgency about that.

I also contacted my friend Diane in Indiana, USA. She had been with me in Egypt multiple times and I wanted to debrief with her about the last five weeks. To my surprise, she seemed concerned about this new virus. She even said that she thought I should come home immediately.

I had no intention of doing that, but rather than flat out deny what she had said, I told her I would think about it. It was just a nice way to move on to the other things I wanted to chat with her about.

After her call, I followed through with my promise to her and tuned in to my inner guidance. I was given the suggestion to look at the options to change my flight home.

Hmm... That was interesting. So I followed that guidance, thinking maybe I would leave one day early or something like that.

As I started researching, I saw that Lufthansa (my airline home) was offering free flight changes. No penalties. Hmmm...

It was like following the bread crumbs. Bit by bit I was gently guided into changing my flight to Wednesday morning at 3:00 am. That gave me just one day to play with the kids. Not what I had planned at all.

But throughout the whole process of changing the flight, I was following my inner guidance. Knowing that I could trust it, and that I was following it well, gave me a sense of peace and sureness. I knew what I was doing was the best thing.

I did not know exactly *why* it was best, but I felt *sure* that what I had chosen was the best thing to do.

Having spent multiple decades actively learning how to recognize this guidance (through making both good and bad choices), I now had a skill that served me very well.

So early Wednesday morning on March 11, 2020, I boarded my flight from Cairo to Germany and later connected to my flight back to Boston in the USA. Everything went smoothly. It was my easiest transatlantic flight yet. The airports in Cairo, Munich and Boston were all practically empty, which made things very easy.

I arrived at 5:00 pm, Boston time, where a ride was waiting for me. At 6:00 pm that day the borders were closed. Only US citizens were allowed to enter the country, which meant that the following flights from Germany (with their German staff) were cancelled.

If I had waited even one more day, I would have been stuck in Cairo with no way to get home (the direct flights to the US were also cancelled), or in Germany where I had nowhere to stay.

The relief I felt was enormous. And that was compounded as I watched the chaos that ensued at the US airports in the days that followed. I had very narrowly missed being trapped in a horrible nightmare.

By contrast, I had a smooth, easy journey home and I also felt a deep peace within myself during the whole trip because I was sure that what I was doing was the best thing.

All of this left me with a feeling that I wanted to share this skill – the ability to discern what to do when it isn't so easy to know. I wished all those people living the airport nightmares in the following days knew how to tune in when they needed it. So that is how the determination to write this book was born.

It's Not Just the Big Stuff

When people think about listening for spiritual help, there is the idea that this does not include all the small choices we make every day – all those mundane difficulties we have to deal with on a daily basis.

I remember an Episcopalian priest saying to me that he didn't think it was right to pray and ask for help with finding your contact lens.

Isn't that a pity? God is evidently too busy with things like world hunger to take out some time to help you find that contact lens you dropped.

This idea is ridiculous in multiple ways. For starters, it assumes that the only one listening to your prayers is the Almighty God of the Universe. What about all the many, many helpers of different sorts just waiting around to step up and assist you? As one friend likes to say, "No unemployed angels!"

Secondly, one of the basic spiritual principles is that size does not count. It could be a penny* on the ground in front of you or a big lottery win. From the spiritual perspective, both are simply a lucky increase in the amount of money you have. As the saying goes, "You can come to the ocean with a bucket or a teacup. The ocean doesn't care."

When people have their life reviews in near-death experiences or past-life regressions, they are often surprised to find that the most wonderful thing they did during their lives was that time they smiled at a stranger. From the spiritual perspective, it is the purity of our actions that is recorded, not our idea about the magnitude of their importance.

So whether we think the issue is big or small, the helpful, loving guidance is here to assist us with finding our contact lenses, as well as sorting out our emotional difficulties and tough choices.

This book focuses on the skills of interpreting your inner intuitive knowing and accessing all kinds of guidance through writing. When these two skills become part of your everyday vocabulary, you will find that you can quickly "tune in" with more and more ease.

If you have already been working on this, these exercises can make your connections even easier and faster.

****

*If you are now asking or praying for more monetary abundance, how you respond to that penny delivers a message about how well you receive money in general. Celebration and gratitude will keep it coming!

CHAPTER TWO

Inner Knowing

How Does It Feel When It's Right?

An endless stream of thoughts goes through our minds each day. Some of them are replays from something we heard or thought before, some are observations about what we are encountering in that moment, some are chains of associations that lead from one thing to another – sort of like going on YouTube to watch a quick video you are interested in and an hour later...

In his lectures about how neuropathways develop in our brains, Joe Dispenza often says that the great majority of our everyday thoughts are the habitual-recycling kind. We have a whole history of beliefs that come from our past. These may not be true at all, but they keep repeating in our minds until we evaluate whether or not they are actually true.

For example, I was told as a child, "Never wear green and blue together. They clash." Oh really? Does that mean the green trees clash with the sky? And, "Never wear brown and black together." Uh-oh. What shall I tell my beautiful brown horse that has a black tail and mane?

Black Shoe Polish

It was Christmas time. My sister and I (now adults) came home to my parent's house for the holidays. We both lived in other parts of the country, so it was a treat to be together and have some fun sister-time. It was decided that we *needed* to go out shopping "for just a few more items" before Christmas. Time for Girls-Go-Shopping!

We chose one of the big stores where you can find most anything and our primal hunter-gatherer instincts went into high gear. We were scouting out the best bargains and looking for those special things that would make Christmas morning lots more fun.

In typical girl-shopping mode, we were searching for things separately but in close enough proximity that we could triumphantly show what we found to the other with a proud exclamation, "Look what I found! So cute, and what a great price!"

At one point I found myself in an aisle alone and noticed there was black shoe polish there. It really attracted my attention for some reason. I was about to call out to my sister, "Look! They have black shoe polish!" But my next thought was, "That's ridiculous. Of course they have black shoe polish. What's so special about that?" I even felt sort of silly for having thought to say it. I forgot it and kept looking around for other things.

We continued our shopping, checked out, and left the store with all our wonderful bargains. Back in the car, we had been driving about five minutes when my sister said, "Oh, darn! I forgot to get black shoe polish! That was the one thing I really needed."

So from that moment on that became what my sister and I call a "Black Shoe Polish Moment." It's when your intuition was giving you a helpful clue, but you rationalized it away or ignored it.

Have you had something like that happen, too? Maybe you were packing for a trip and suddenly thought of putting in a light-weight summer shirt, but then your logical mind came in with, "No, it won't be that warm in March," only to have an unseasonable heat wave come through when you got there, and boy, did you wish you had that lightweight shirt.

Which is it?

If we want to have better intuition or to develop a deep, reliable connection to wise inner knowing, we need ways to distinguish the different sorts of thoughts that come into our heads. So how do we know the difference between real intuition and all these other thoughts?

Good News and Bad News

There is both good news and bad news about that question. The good news is that those helpful thoughts *do* already occur to you. You may not be aware of them as such, but they are definitely there. With that in mind, the question becomes how to recognize them?

The bad news is that this is a skill. The way skills are developed is by doing something and finding out if that worked or not. It's the "or not" part that can hold people back because that means it will involve having failures.

So, the uncomfortable truth is that the way intuition and reliable inner knowing are developed is TRIAL AND ERROR.

Flavors and Reliability

If you are going to make choices based on your intuition or inner knowing, it needs to be reliable. In religious doctrine this is called having *faith*. For people like myself, having faith in something without having experienced any proof is not an option.

All of the following exercises will be ways for you to actually have your own experiences of things either working or not working. That way, the confidence you will have is based on multiple personal experiences – that's what is real to you. It won't be based on something someone else told you.

As you go through these first exercises, what you are looking for is **what clues you into whether it is a valid intuitive thought or not. What are the indicators?**

In the same way as you learned to distinguish the flavors of different foods, the skill is in learning to "taste" the flavor of the valid information. Peppermint ice cream and vanilla ice cream are both ice cream. They may even look the same, but you can tell the difference when you taste them. You have lots of thoughts (ice cream) but they have different "flavors" to them.

The more sophisticated your tasting abilities are, the more confidence you will have with whether the impressions you are getting are reliable – was that peppermint or spearmint ice cream? Psychics and mediums, who work with this kind of information all the time, each develop their own unique inner vocabulary of what they can rely on.

So, as you do these exercises, you will be developing your own personal way of knowing which thoughts are the intuitive ones. You'll be able to recognize them by their flavor. And along with that, there will be inner feelings that will help make it clear, too.

You probably do this to a certain extent already. These exercises will just make what you've already got even better!

Are These Statements True?

Think about the following statements and notice how you know if they are true or not.

1. You have 11 fingers.
2. People always tell the truth.
3. You are hungry right now.

Let's look at each one.

1. You already have decided how many fingers you have. If you have any doubt, you can easily count them. This is something that should not need any discussion. It's obvious.
2. You have had the experience of knowing someone did not tell the truth. That person might even be you yourself. So, you have a personal experience that proves this statement is false. You are sure about that because you have your own personal proof from your own life.
3. To find out if you are hungry right now, you probably had to check in with your body in the present moment to see how you were feeling. You may say, "My body is always hungry. I always want to eat." But the only way to know *for sure* is to notice how you feel in this exact moment. Maybe by some strange miracle, you *don't* actually feel hungry right now. Or it could be the opposite. You think during this part of the day you couldn't be hungry, but maybe you are. The only way to know is to check right now and see how you feel inside.

Number three is the important one here. The obvious things, like your fingers, are not things you need your intuition for. If you already know from past experience (like whether everyone tells the truth) you also don't need any special intuitive insight.

The third question (about hunger) is closest to how you can access your inner guidance system. Here are the similarities.

1. Intuitive knowledge only exists in the exact present moment. It is not from the past.
2. In order to perceive the information correctly, you need to allow any answer to emerge, all options need to be allowed. Outguessing the answer by referencing your past thoughts will not give you an accurate response. Any previous assumptions (like, "I'm always hungry," or "I won't be hungry at this time of day") will interfere. They clog up the airways.

If you want good guidance right now, it means putting your focus on your present experience (not your past ideas) and not having preconceptions about what the answer should or might be.

Good Yes/No Questions

Another component is which questions you ask. **Simple, direct, and honest** are good rules to follow whenever asking for guidance.

Example: Let's imagine someone named Helen wants to know if she should quit her job.

Most of us have developed a self-image by the time we reach adulthood. We do our best to think thoughts that go along with that image. Almost like composing lines for a character in a play, the self-image character we have constructed is supposed to act, talk, and even *think* in a certain way. This can carry over into how we phrase our questions.

Helen thinks of herself as a reasonable, responsible, kind person who wants the best for everyone. She believes the problems she has at work are because of the other people who work there. She wants to get an answer from her intuition about whether to quit her job. How might she phrase her question?

Should I quit my job? I think maybe it's not good for me, but I want to do whatever is the right thing. It really isn't good for me to be there anymore, but my father will be mad if I quit. He always said not to be a quitter. The people at that job are just not good for me to be around.

What do you notice about this question? It appears to be a yes or no question, but it is not so simple. There are a number of assumptions and beliefs that are intertwined with it.

If Helen has developed an ability to dialogue with a helpful spirit guide, they could probably help her work through the various components – worries about what her father will think, blaming the difficulties on her coworkers without seeing her own role in it, and her desire to do "whatever is the right thing."

Without first working through these added components, Helen won't be able to readily embrace either the yes or the no answer. She won't feel at peace with either one.

You can probably see how this sort of question will not be good for practicing how to distinguish which are yes and no answers.

The best questions to practice on are the ones where we don't have any additional agendas pulling us one way or another, and where the consequences of the choices are not so important. If possible, it's also good to discern if the question we ask is something that perpetuates the image we want to have of ourselves but isn't actually how we really feel deep down.

Here are a few experiments to try. The goal is to develop your ability to **get the "flavor" of the thoughts** that give you the correct yes or no answers.

1. Calling a Friend

Before making the call, stop (literally, stop moving your body, freeze). Take three long, easy breaths and then ask, "Would this be a good time to call _____?" Wait for either a *yes* or a *no*.

There will be more ways to check for *yes* and *no* later, but for now, just try leaving a space and wait until either a *yes* or *no* pops into your mind.

Acknowledge the answer by saying what you got out loud ("yes/no"). Then say, "Thank you." This is a good policy for any guidance you get. If you don't appreciate what comes to you, what makes you think you will get more?

If the answer was a *no*...

Go back in your mind and try to remember exactly how the *no* felt. Did it have a certain tempo to it? Was it quick or slow? Did you hear it in your mind? If so, what was the tone of the voice in your mind? Was it matter-of-fact, urgent, tentative, loud, soft? Was there a certain kind of feeling in your body? Were there any particular sensations that came with it? Did your body feel heavy or light? Did you see any images or colors in your mind?

Next, give a **one-sentence answer to this question, "How would you describe what happened as you got the answer?"** Describe it to yourself in the words that make sense to you. This is for your own reference.

If you got a *yes*, the process is the same.

Next, make the call. If you got a *yes* and there is no answer, then that gives you the information that what you were getting was not correct. Trial and error!

If you got a *yes* and your friend answers. Ask, "Is this a good time for you to chat?" Again, notice from the tone of their voice if it is a good time or not.

Whichever way it goes, you are gathering information about how to judge if you are getting correct answers or not. Remember that part of the learning process is that you need to get both right and wrong answers (so that you can learn to tell the difference).

2. Receiving a Phone Call

When your phone rings, you can also try a yes/no. This time the question is, "Is that a call I want to take?" You won't have time to do three breaths, but just ask yourself that and see what you get. If you get a *yes*, go ahead and answer the phone. Was your answer correct? Whichever way it came out, write down your one-sentence description.

You can also try asking yourself who it is that is calling.

3. Mail Delivery

If your mail arrives at different times each day, that is another yes/no question you could ask yourself. "Has the mail arrived yet today?" Make a choice and then say your answer out loud.

Why is it worthwhile to say the answers you are getting out loud? Part of working with the unseen world is making that which we normally cannot perceive into something which we can. If you don't want to say it out loud for some reason, write it down. Both ways, you are committing to what your answer is. Then it is to find out whether it was right or not.

What makes doing these exercises worthwhile is learning what you can trust. You will build that by checking how it felt when you got the yes or no. What was the flavor of it and how did you feel as you received it?

Think about what other things in your daily life that you could use for yes/no practice.

Building Reliability

The three exercises above are all ways that you can begin to develop a sense of whether the information that either pops into your mind, or that you feel somehow in your body, is reliable or not. If you never experiment, you won't get to have any sureness. This book seeks to give you tools you can use to develop confidence with this in your daily life. It is not about fantasy or things you might like to believe. It needs to be real.

The only way to have it be real is to experiment and get good at evaluating when it worked and when it did not. This is not about convincing yourself of anything. It is about finding things out.

Once you get the idea of how doing these tests can work, you will probably find other things in your daily life that you can use for your experiments.

Invocations or Prayers

Depending on what your belief system is, you may find that saying a little prayer or invocation before you ask the questions is effective. This is a personal thing, so it is for each one of us to find our own unique way with it. Whatever works for you is the best thing to do! Results are what matter.

Keeping Track

One part of the processes above was to put the "tasting" experience into a one sentence description. Keeping a log of these descriptions will bring you a lot of benefit. Descriptions of the ones that were successful are the important ones to write in your log book, but the failed ones can be helpful as well.

Why is this important? Our minds like security. That security comes from staying within what is familiar. Anything outside of that takes extra energy to deal with. A very common experience for those who are working on expanding themselves is to learn something new – this is so wonderful and exciting, yes! – and then a week or two later it is gone. The knowing, the feelings, the understandings that were so clear and wonderful, all gone.

To get it back requires additional focus and energy, so many times the great improvements that were made are lost.

The key to retaining these new abilities and understandings is to bring them into your everyday, 3D world in as many ways as possible. When people refer to "castles in the air," this is a way to describe that which stays in the ethers and does not become a living physical-life reality. Anything you can do to make your new experiences physical will help you retain them.

Writing something down does just this. What was only a thought (nonphysical) has now become a marked piece of paper (physical matter). You can now say, just like you may have read in the Bible, "It is written..."

Reviewing your notes, especially before sleeping, is also a good way to integrate the information.

Telling a friend is another way to begin to own any new insights. However, when you are in the learning-collecting-trial-and-error stage with something new, talking with someone else about it means that their reactions to what you are doing will become part of the experience for you. You may find that you want to keep that complication out of it until it has gelled for you.

For people who like having a buddy for their activities, an "experimenting-partner" can make working on the exercises more fun and exciting.

Stay Away from Predictions

At this point, it is suggested that you stay away from trying to predict things in the future. This can add in a bunch of components that will cloud your results.

For example, if you try to get the winning lottery numbers, there will be multiple ramifications if you win. Many lottery winners suffer as a result of winning. Your helpful guides and angels may be wanting to protect you from that outcome. So, asking for information like that – things that will have a big impact on your life – is not a good way to do these experiments. The goal of these exercises is to develop your intuitive abilities and connections.

Using experiments like phone calls is good because whether you are right or wrong doesn't have an impact on your life in general. The results are just for the experiments themselves.

Yes/No Answers

Here are some suggestions about ways to distinguish if it is a *yes* or *no*.

1. Traffic Light

Imagine a traffic light in your mind. Is it red, green, or yellow? Another one is a STOP sign.

2. Someone You Respect

- Picture someone you respect in your mind. A person whose advice you would value.
- See their face in your mind's eye, think of your question, and ask it in your mind.
- How do they react? Are they nodding or shaking their head? Smiling or frowning?

3. Weighing It Up

- Use your two hands as the yes and no. You can also imagine a symbol for each option that you are considering. Put a symbol in each hand.
- Next, close your eyes and move your hands up and down alternatively. In other words, one hand goes up while the other goes down. Just move them a bit like you had two things in your hands and you were estimating which was heavier.
- With your eyes still closed, let your hands stop doing the motion (while still keeping them out in front of you).
- Open your eyes and see which hand is higher and which is lower. There is your answer.

4. Listening to Your Heart

- Place your hand on your heart. Let it rest there for a few moments and feel the sense of peace that comes to you.
- Gently tap on your heart and chest area a few times. This helps your focus to go there.

- Remember that your heart has its own brain of sorts and has its own way of thinking. You might also repeat to yourself, "My heart knows."
- Remember what your question is and ask that question while you keep your focus on your heart. Your heart will speak in its own way. It is different than the thoughts in your head. Finding what that language is for you is like coming home to your true self.

For more about listening to your heart and some of the current science about the heart's "brain," look up the *Heart Math Institute*.

5. Tilt Test

- Stand with your eyes closed.
- Think of your question and ask it out loud or in your mind. Say the question at least 3-4 times, more may be needed.
- Your body will begin to lean forward or backward. It may be slight, but that is all you need.

Forward is *yes*, backward is *no*.

6. Reading Your Voice

Put your two options (yes/no or two alternatives) into one word each or a very short phrase.

Example using yes or no: Say "Yes, (pause), yes, (pause), yes."

- Notice the sound of your voice. If you heard someone saying it like that would you believe them? Are they telling the truth? Do you sound relaxed and peaceful with what you are saying? Does it sound like you are forcing it or trying to sound like you mean something that you do not?

- Notice what you feel in your body as you hear your voice saying that. Do you get a sinking feeling? A clutching in your stomach? Does your body feel heavier? Do you feel happy energy lifting you up? Do you want to lean forward or back? Was there an involuntary sigh when you finished speaking?
- Did you get any visuals as you heard the word being repeated? Colors? Images? Memories?

Next, do the same thing with "No."

You can also use your smartphone to record yourself speaking the short phrase (3 times with pauses) and then listen to yourself like you are listening to someone else to see if they are telling the truth.

7. Muscle Testing

You can read about muscle testing online and watch some videos about how to do it. There are different versions. Some require two people (the other person tests the strength of your arm while it is extended). You can do it alone by making an O with two fingers and testing how strong that is with two fingers on the other hand. Recommendation: Dr. Bradley Nelson.

This is handy for daily decisions – would it be good to eat this or that, should I turn left or right, am I driving the right direction?

8. Using a Pendulum

Being able to get reliable results with a pendulum can be handy. I myself use it to replace the muscle testing while working with the Emotion Code chart. It is also good when helping other people ferret out what issues are blocking them.

The caution with using the pendulum, however, is that it is very good at reading your own mind. If you have even the slightest opinion about what you imagine the answer might be, the pendulum can easily simply reflect back to you what you already believe or what you would like the answer to be.

For example, a friend sees a dress in a store that she would like to have. The price is much higher than her budget. Buying it would not be good for her financially, so if she was not having any emotions about the dress, she would know that buying it that day was not a good thing to do.

However, she is swept up in the enthusiasm of the moment and is now just looking for a good excuse to override her wiser choice.

She pulls out her pendulum and asks, "Should I buy this dress?"

What do you suppose the answer is? Her subconscious will give her the answer she already has decided she wants.

Note: The pendulum is a good tool to use when **sending energy or prayers to another person**.

- On a piece of paper, write what you would like to broadcast to the other person.
- Draw a heart shape around that (love is your phone line).
- Place your pendulum over the words in the heart and begin your prayers or distant healing. The pendulum will begin to spin around like the blades of a helicopter.
- Continue to maintain your prayerful healing focus until the pendulum stops spinning. When it does, that indicates that the right amount of energy has been sent.
- Put the pendulum down and make your prayers of thanks and gratitude.

Next Steps

Once you feel that you are able to pretty reliably discern if you are getting a *yes* or *no* for things, you may feel ready to "up the ante" a bit. Increasing the challenges will increase the areas that your inner knowing will be useful, BUT the errors (remember it will still always be trial and error) will begin to have a cost.

Keeping the Error-Cost Down

At one point, I was ready to put my intuitive inner knowing to the test. "Let's get real here." I had started to invest in stocks, so I thought this would be a good way to see if I was willing to really believe in the inner guidance I had been developing. Something that involves your own money gets very real, very fast.

I tried a number of different methods. I would look at the charts of different stocks and try to imagine if the line that showed their values would go up or down.

I checked in with myself in ways as were listed in the yes/no exercises above. As I made a purchase I watched myself to see how I felt inside (making note of the "flavor").

Then I had to wait and see whether my predictions were correct or not. This was quite instructive, but also time-consuming. The feedback about how correct I was took time.

The other detraction was that this created some emotional tension because there were always potential (and not just potential, but *real*) financial losses involved.

Free Cell Game

Later, I came up with a better way to improve my skills. What I wanted was to be able to function in my everyday life with a feeling that I was "right on track." There is a wonderful feeling of confidence, ease, and clarity that makes everything we do in life easier and more pleasant. As an example, I was in that state on the return trip from Cairo to Boston (pages 9-12).

Knowing whether a certain stock will increase my money was certainly nice, but *living* in a state of harmonious flow was something I valued even more. It's a feeling like everything is okay. Julian of Norwich said, "All is well, all is well." Isn't it nice when we feel that way?

And when we add to that all-is-well feeling a *knowing just what to do next.* Isn't that even better? That was the state I wanted to reach on an ongoing basis.

So how to get there?

First of all, I needed the knowledge that it *is* possible to step into that flow. My own experiences with my spiritual work through decades of healing and channeling energies had already shown me that. But how to live it in an everyday way, not just when I am in a highly spiritually attuned state? I needed a way to practice.

Enter a little game I play on my tablet or phone, the FreeCell Solitaire app (I use the MobilityWare version). The reason this particular game is so useful is that the only chance that is involved is how the cards get laid out at the very beginning.

After that, whether you win or get stuck is entirely based on THE CHOICES YOU MAKE. This is exactly what I needed. Immediate feedback on the choices I made.

Staying On Track

After playing the game now thousands of times, I can promise you that *there is always a way to win it.* If you get stuck there is a back arrow that takes you back step by step to the beginning.

When I first started playing, I used the approach of asking my inner guidance which card to move next. I did this for every single move. I was also monitoring myself as I did that to see if I began to go into a state of *mental reasoning*. The state of being guided and the state of mental reasoning were mutually exclusive for me. If I went into trying to figure it out, I no longer functioned in the flow of the *stream of inner knowing*.

I worked at it a long time and eventually got so that I was winning on the first try each time. That was nice, but somehow it made me feel insignificant. Was I just a robot?

In the next stage, I tried a different modality. I would try playing the game without any inner help. If I got stuck, then I would tune in and get the help needed to make the game work out.

That was kind of nice, but it didn't serve me all that well. It was like crawling along and then if I got into trouble asking someone to help me stand up so that I could walk.

That stage culminated in a game that I could not get to work. Again and again, I went back and started over. There is a stopwatch that shows the playing time for each game, and after more than an hour, I set it aside. When I came back later, I kept at it for another hour and still couldn't get it to work. Sigh... When I am on track, winning a game is usually less than three minutes.

So, one more time, I went back to the beginning. I waited for guidance to make each move. Presto! It all worked out. And then I just laughed and laughed. And I am sure the angels were all laughing with me. I saw how very silly and obstinate I was to want to do it all myself. It was like a little kid that says, "Me do it!" Hahaha!

After that, I tried a new method. Instead of having a blank personality that just functioned by being instructed or the other mode where I tried to do it all myself and only asked for help when under duress, I wanted a new mode that would honor and include all parties. That is the one I am presently working with.

I begin by intending to function in the flow while also allowing that flow to mix with the thoughts in my mind. This is more like canoeing on a river. You are in the flow, but also making little decisions along the way.

If I get stuck, that means I stepped out of the river at some point. If I was alert to the texture of the flow-experience, I can go back in my mind and notice when I stepped out of it. Often, I just need to go back two or three moves to the place I remember having a slight feeling of doubt.

It's this *being on track* feeling, or *being in tune,* that has become the flavor that I strive to function in throughout my normal activities each day.

Phone Calls

One way you can begin to develop this "being right in the flow" state is by sensing when a telephone conversation is complete. If the person you are speaking with is also attuned, you will both recognize the moment that your conversation would best finish. You both sense that feeling of completion and can then move into gratitude to have had the opportunity to speak together. No one feels shortchanged or interrupted.

Highlighting

One method I used for choosing the next card in the FreeCell game was highlighting. This is when you scan a series of objects and one of them somehow looks brighter to you. It is as though your intuition is pointing at that particular one.

If you remember the Black Shoe Polish story (page 7-8), this is what was happening when I was in the shoe polish aisle. You may have had this happen at a bookstore. You look at a shelf of books and there is one that just seems to pop out at you. Sometimes those books even fall right off the shelf!

Body Pointing

Another way that our intuition (or helpful angels or guides) can point things out to us is by actually moving our body in a way that we notice something. You might find that you have turned your head a bit and you are now looking at something, not something you thought of ahead of time. It "just sort of happened."

You might even think, "Why am I looking at that right now?" That's a good question to ask, because you may well then get an answer! We are probably being guided in this way much more than we realize.

Now that this body pointing has been mentioned here, you may notice that it is actually happening with you multiple times a day.

Pay special attention if you are about to leave the house. There may be things that you need to take with you – like your cellphone that you thought was in your purse but actually was taken out and it is now on the table. Those little movements that turn your head or eyes a certain way are trying to help you out. Why do you suppose you found yourself staring at the gas gauge or oven that was left on?

This can also be very handy if you have misplaced your car keys!

Hits and Nudges

My friends and I will often say, "I got a hit to call Janice yesterday..." A *hit* is a short way to say that something popped into our minds that would be a good idea to do. Some people also call it "getting a nudge."

What usually happens is that a person or idea will somehow come into your awareness "out of the blue." This will often happen when you are doing a mundane task and your mind is free of focused thought. People get these in the shower, on the toilet, upon waking in the morning, driving in the car, washing the dishes, any time they aren't busily focused on a task or talking with someone.

Again, how they show up is different for everyone. It could be an image in your mind, something you hear in your head, a feeling you get, a memory... The most notable thing about these is that they are not the result of a particular train of thought you were already engaged in. They come into your mind unexpectedly.

Once that has happened, you can use one of the processes suggested before to test if acting on the idea is a good one (example, "Calling a Friend," page 14).

****

See Chapter 7 for ways to get confirmations.

CHAPTER THREE

Writing Tools

Creating a Place to Receive, Streams, Truths, and Other Writing Exercises

You are probably reading this book hoping to gain a better "phone line" to some wise and helpful guidance. The last chapter covered ways to get yes/no answers to questions, as well as highlighting, body pointing, and intuitive hits or nudges that can lead you in good directions. But wouldn't it be nice to actually be able to have a good sit-down talk with some wise and helpful being that could explain things to you in everyday language?

These next chapters go into how to do just that.

Creating the Vessel

The first step to *having* something is to create a vessel to hold it in. If you want to have some water nearby so that you can have a drink whenever you are thirsty, that water needs to be in a glass, cup, or bottle – a vessel to hold it there for you. If you want to receive text messages, you need a device and a personal number/address where you can receive those.

If you want to have a good, uninterrupted, private conversation with someone, you need to have the time, a place that is private, and a way to put a halt on the interruptions. Those elements create the vessel for your high-quality conversation.

Likewise, if you want to converse with a wise spirit guide or teacher, once you make the time and have the receptivity that is needed, writing can create the vessel (the place) for the communications you desire.

Formless into Form

When the Divine touches us in ways that we can perceive – with words we understand, physical touch and sensations, sounds we hear... - we feel we have been met. God is with us. The angels are around us. Our loved ones are still here.

When those experiences are missing, we can feel we are alone. There is no one and nothing "out there" for us. And nothing here to help us at all. So, for things to be REAL for us, we crave an experience that is perceived by our five senses. As the expression goes, "That's where the rubber hits the road."

The challenge with spiritual communication is that there needs to be a sort of "translation" from *that which is not physical, linear, or limited* into our physical, linear, limited experience of the world, the stuff our five senses perceive.

Full-out spiritual experiences happen beyond thought. They are "beyond the beyond" with no way to adequately describe them.

Those experiences are, of course, incomparably valuable, but they do not necessarily help us with the difficulties and challenges of our daily lives. We also may not glean any particular insights or knowledge from them. To get the value in our everyday lives, we need to somehow translate it into something our linear minds can follow.

As we write down the words that come through the inspired writing, we are doing just that. It becomes physical form, something that has substance and reality to us.

A Skill that Keeps Improving

Because the *non-form into form* process is like translating between two different languages, the result is going to be influenced by the translator. At first that "translator" will have a limited vocabulary, which will make the translations a bit crude. But that is just a start.

As your "vocabulary" (your ability to more accurately perceive the messages) improves, the translations will get more and more accurate. Remember that even a poor translation can be far better than none at all.

Where and When Will You Do Your Writing?

Some people like to have a particular journal or notebook that is dedicated to their explorations with the spiritual communications. As one person put it, "I wouldn't want to mix that up with all the junk in my dump-journal."

Deciding where you will write the exercises in this book is a good idea. The more we act out of *choice* rather than functioning in a default mode, the more capable and empowered we are in our lives. It is a gift we give ourselves.

Another thing you may want to consider is whether you will incorporate this writing into a regular practice – daily, weekly, or with a writing buddy. Most people find that if there isn't regularity with things, it is hard to maintain the momentum.

Choosing to do the writing in the same location can also help with getting into your desired state more quickly.

Creating a Receptive State

Once you have created the vessel by setting aside some time, getting your writing materials together, and settling into a place where you will not easily be disturbed, it's time to begin.

Some people like to do a prayer or invocation that creates a sacred space within which to work. If it feels important to them to do so, that may also include a prayer of protection.

Statement of Intent

It is important to begin by making a statement of your intent for the day. Make it clear, concise, and honest. You can use the following questions as a way to clarify this.

- Why are you doing this?
  Example: *My life isn't working and I don't know why.*
  Example: *I want to get good at hearing clear guidance.*

- What would you like to receive?
  Example: *Today I want to hear any helpful teachings, whatever would be good for me.*
  Example: *I want help on my financial situation.*
  Example: *I want some advice about my marriage.*

- What you are open to, not open to?
  Example: *I only want those who are loving, wise, and helpful.*
  Example: *I want to know what is deep inside myself, including things I don't know about yet.*
  Example: *I need help. I want someone to help me.*

Write it out. Speaking it aloud gives it additional power. By writing and saying your intent out loud, you are doing an action which coincides with your willingness to know.

Commitments and Free Will

You have probably had the experience of someone promising to do something, but then not following through. Our actions are what count. In this case, actually doing your part by discerning what you want and then making that desire physical (writing it down), you are committing yourself to the process.

There is a spiritual law that those in spirit cannot violate our free will. This is one reason why it is so important we ourselves say that we want something. Our saying that translates to us giving our free-will permission for it to be gifted to us.

The First Writing Exercises

The exercises in this chapter will give you a number of tools to pave the way for the communications in the following chapters. They are tools that you can use later to get yourself into the modes that will enable certain kinds of guidance to come through for you.

The writing exercises in this chapter are explorations into what your everyday mind can tap into.

Here is a list of the ones to follow.

- **Stream of Consciousness**
- **Truth-Telling**
- **Reporting an Issue in Nonspecific Language**
- **Explain It to a Child**
- **Storytelling**
- **Writing in the Third Person**

Doing the Exercises in Order

You can, of course, do the following writing exercises in any order you choose. However, they are laid out in Chapters 3-6 in a sequence that is designed to quickly and easily expand your ability to hear and connect with helpful guidance. In the same way that to learn multiplication, you first learn to add, these first exercises open certain pathways and give you what you will need to later access the more subtle communications.

Widening Your View

In the sport of basketball, the way you score is to get the ball into a basket that is elevated in the air. Either it goes into that basket (score!) or it does not. With baseball, a person hits a ball that is thrown to them. If there was a basket somewhere in the outfield and the ball needed to land exactly in that basket, it would be very hard to score. However, in baseball, the ball can land anywhere within a larger area that is considered "in play."

Likewise, when we are asking for guidance, it is useful to expand the area of what we are receiving. Simply widening our views by being receptive to *other points of view* – even the ones that are not so high-level* – helps us to see/hear, those more profound pearls of wisdom when they come to us. Our phone lines need to be open for that to happen.

You may think asking your dog about whether you should break up with your boyfriend doesn't make much sense, but getting your dog's opinion might actually be helpful.

Your dog thinks you are a wonderful, important person. He sees how your boyfriend treats you and whether or not your boyfriend acknowledges how important and special you are. Doggy's opinion might turn out to be the wisest one of all!

Writing with Eyes Closed

After doing the following exercises in the normal way, you might like to try them with eyes closed. Using large paper will make that easier. You can use a sleep mask to block the light out, close your eyes, or turn out the lights in a dark room. You can also try drawing that way, too.

---

*Note that Chapters 5 and 7 cover the importance of discernment with who and what you are connecting to in the *wider reality*.

Stream of Consciousness

The Stream of Consciousness exercise is a good one to start with because it loosens things up and gets us out of our normal thought patterns.

If you already knew how to handle everything in your life and were confident you were making all the best choices as you went along, you probably would not think to reach for additional information.

So, a good first step is to open up *alternate pathways,* alternate ways for your mind to function.

Inspiration and wisdom are a constant option, but we tend to override those with the voices we hear both outside ourselves and within our own minds.

If we are constantly listening to what meditation teachers call our "mind chatter" or "monkey mind" – the recycling of the thoughts of others, our own beliefs from the past, or worries about the future – it can be hard for a helpful guardian angel or guide to get a word in edgewise!

There is a passage in the Bible (1 Kings 19:11-13) where it says that God was not the strong wind that tore the mountains and broke the rocks in pieces, not an earthquake, not a fire. Instead, He spoke to Elijah as "a still small voice."

Many meditation techniques and spiritual practices have been developed to help us get past the mind chatter. In meditation, one may be encouraged to simply let the thoughts that arise pass by without giving them attention. This *Stream of Consciousness* exercise works with the mind chatter in a different way.

STREAM OF CONSCIOUSNESS STEPS

1. Get a stack of paper. Scrap paper that has something you no longer need on the opposite side is good. You won't be needing a lot of these sheets after the exercise is completed.

2. Take one sheet and write down a question about something that is bothering you or where you need to decide something. Put that sheet aside in a place you can easily get it again.

Examples:

- Dealing with a difficult situation
  "How should I deal with _____ (that difficult coworker)?"

- Buying a particular item
  "Should I get the Subaru, the Toyota, or something else?"

- Participating in an upcoming activity
  "Should I go to the party on Friday?"

The subject can be anything you want some help or clarity on.

Make it as simple and to the point as possible. The best is if the question is the same way that you would think it in your head.

For example, "Should I go to the party on Friday?" is better than trying to ask it in what you might think is a more correct way to ask. "Would going to the party on Friday be the most beneficial thing for me to do that day?"

3. Begin with 5-10 sheets of paper, depending on how large you write and whether it is lined or not.

Make an unshakable agreement with yourself that you are going to write continuously and fill all of the pages you have in front of you. You will not stop until all the pages are filled with writing.

4. Begin writing each word that comes into your mind. It does not matter what the words are or if they make sense. If your mind says, "I can't think of anything," write on the paper, "I CAN'T THINK OF ANYTHING."

If your mind continues, "I still can't think of anything," then write that down, too.

Keep writing that (just write the words over and over) until another thought comes into your mind. This "I can't think of anything" is just a ruse by the mind to keep you blocked.

It is not true. Your mind constantly has thoughts going through it. It may pause briefly when you are fully engaged in some activity (like riding a rollercoaster), but that non-thinking does not last long.

If you suddenly realize that you forgot to return a phone call. Write that down, but don't stop. Remember, you made an agreement with yourself to do this. It's important to follow through.

At first it may seem silly, but that is not the point at all. The important thing is that by writing down every single thought that comes into your mind you are interrupting the status quo in your mind. Part of that is because these thoughts are now being recorded.

But even more important than that, you are now creating a vessel, an opportunity, for *an expansion of your thoughts*. If your thoughts have fallen into a pattern that created a deep narrow stream in your mind, this exercise makes room for a big, beautiful river to flow freely there.

Words, Images, Sounds, Smells, Memories

The words you are writing do not need to be complete thoughts in sentences. They can be words that have no context but simply pop into your mind. They can also be images. You might see a dog in your mind. You would then write the word DOG.

You may hear a sound or remember a sound. Write that down, too. Maybe the lyrics to a song come drifting into your mind. Just keep recording whatever you think of.

If memories come up, try to write them down in just a few words, like a reference, not telling the whole story because getting into the story mode will activate a different part of your mind.

Some people even get smells – cookies in the oven or lilacs in the spring. Those often have associations. Write the smell and the associations, too, but *don't start to invent it*.

This is not about being inventive and fanciful. This is to simply record the thoughts that are playing like a soundtrack in your head or what you see in your mind's eye.

5. When your sheets of paper are all filled up, reach for the question you wrote on the original sheet that you laid aside.

Read the question and go back into the stream of consciousness mode. On that paper, write anything that comes into your mind – words, images, other impressions.

What you have done is you have created an avenue to tap into wisdom within yourself that would normally never get a chance to be heard.

It may feel like the still, small voice within or it may have a different texture to it, but it will be different than the normal way that you think. Give this other voice a chance to speak. *Do not evaluate or analyze.* You can do that later. Now is a time to see what emerges.

Try to keep it light and easy without demanding of yourself that it be deeply profound or something that feels foreign to you. This is within your very self, just a voice that isn't often given the chance to be heard. Just continue the pattern of writing down the words, images, and other impressions coming to you. *No evaluations now.*

6. When you have filled up that paper, keep writing or stop, whichever feels better to you.

7. Go back to the original 5-10 sheets. Read over what you have written. It can be interesting to see what is actually going on in our minds on a daily basis. Is there anything you see there that is worthwhile?

On a new sheet of paper, or in your journal, make some notes of anything you noticed or anything you find there that you would like to remember. Afterwards, you can throw the 5-10 sheets away.

8. Going back to the sheet that has your question on it and the responses that you wrote, now is the time to let your analytical mind evaluate what you have there. What do you find there that is helpful?

9. In your journal, write out the original question again. Then, using your normal analytical thought process, write some instructions to yourself about the best way to handle the situation. What is the best answer to your question?

SHORT VERSION - STREAM OF CONSCIOUSNESS

1. Get a stack of paper.

2. Take one sheet and write down a question about something that is bothering you or something you need to decide. Put that sheet aside.

3. Begin with 5-10 sheets of paper. Make an unshakable agreement with yourself that you are going to write continuously and fill all of the pages you have in front of you. You will not stop until all the pages are filled with writing.

4. Begin writing each word, image, sound, memory, smell... that comes into your mind. The words you are writing do not need to be complete thoughts in sentences. *Don't start to invent it.* You are simply recording what comes into your mind spontaneously.

5. When your sheets of paper are all filled up, reach for the question you wrote on the original sheet that you laid aside. Read the question and go back into writing in the stream of consciousness mode. *Do not evaluate or analyze.*

6. When you have filled up that paper, keep writing or stop, whichever feels better to you.

7. Go back to the original 5-10 sheets. Read over what you have written. In your journal or on a new sheet of paper make some notes of anything you find there that you would like to remember.

8. Going back to the sheet that has your question on it and the responses that you wrote, let your analytical mind evaluate what you have there. What do you find there that is helpful?

9. Copy the original question into your journal. Then, using your normal analytical thought process, write a response. What is the best answer to that question?

Truth-Telling

Making true statements can seem like an easy, *not-so-profound* exercise, but it is not to be underestimated. After all, it is said that "the truth shall set you free," and there is truth in that statement!

If we feel confused about something – we don't know how to handle a situation, what choice to make, what actions to take – it is often because we don't know what the truth is about it. We are missing the information that would make the answer obvious to us.

So, our confusion means there is something which is hidden from us; there is something we are not seeing or understanding. The good news is that the information we need *does* actually exist.

The Universal Internet

As has been proven repeatedly by those doing remote viewing or psychics who find missing persons, information about *everything* exists in the ethers (or the "universal field of consciousness"). It is all accessible to us, IF we are capable of making the connection to it.

In the same way, you might be at a friend's house where there is a strong wifi signal. Your friend knows the password and can access the internet through the wifi, so your friend can tap into all that information.

But you can't access that information if you don't have the password or if you don't have a phone with a data package. If you come from a place where they don't have computers, internet, and wifi, you wouldn't even know that accessing the internet through wifi at your friend's house was even an option.

So how do we tap into this universal field of consciousness where all the information we need resides?

Some people are more gifted than others with these abilities, but the fact is that since *it is there*, we all have the ability, to a greater or lesser extent, to access it.

This truth-telling exercise is one way to increase your ability to tap into it.

Our Own Subconscious

Another lucky thing is that we often actually already have all the information we need in our own subconscious. What happens is that for one reason or another (these reasons are personal to each of us) we have hidden that information from ourselves.

By doing the truth-telling, we communicate to our own subconscious that "Yes, I *do* want to know the truth about this." That opens a doorway for the truth about things to come out into the open.

Doing the Truth-Telling Exercise

For this exercise, one starts with the obvious things that are around you. There is no need to come up with the profound meaning of the universe or anything like that.

The important thing is that the statements be *true*. So, sticking with the easy stuff at the beginning is best.

Note that the statements should be true, *as far as you know*. You do not need to be able to prove them to anyone else. Just *intend* to speak the truth as you write. This is something for yourself. And misspellings also certainly don't matter at all!

TRUTH-TELLING STEPS

1. Write down a question about something that is bothering you or where you need to decide something.

Examples:

- Dealing with a difficult situation
  "How should I deal with _____ (that difficult coworker)?"

- Buying a particular item
- "Should I get the Subaru, the Toyota, or something else?"

- Participating in an upcoming activity
  "Should I go to the party on Friday?"

The subject can be anything where you want some help or clarity. Make it as simple and to the point as possible. The best is if the question is the same way that you would think it in your head.

2. Begin by writing *easy* true statements. Things in your immediate environment are a good place to start.

Examples:

I am sitting down.
I have ten fingers.
I am wearing a red shirt.
I am sitting in front of a window.
Outside that window, I see a tree.

Do this as quickly as possible. Try not to hesitate or overthink your statements. Write one after another without pausing in between. How many true statements can you write in a short period of time? You can even set a timer if you would like.

3. When that gets boring, experiment with making the statements more descriptive. For example, "I am wearing a watch," could become, "There is a device here on my wrist that keeps track of my relationship with the sun."

Remember the goal is to get into the flow of TRUTH.

Doing this exercise is a perfect example of not just saying something but actually *doing it*. You are doing the action of being-in-truth each time you write one of your true statements. This is you saying in essence, "I DO want to know the truth."

4. After you have written a lot of true statements (and as you continue to write them), allow your focus to also include any other thoughts that come into your mind, even if they are not necessarily true statements.

Remember that you set an intent at the beginning of the exercise that you wanted clarity on a particular question. These other thoughts that begin to emerge in your mind may actually be clues that relate to an answer to your question. Therefore, it is good to write these down, as well. Maybe later those clues will make some sense to you.

Remember to keep writing rapidly. No mulling things over as you go along. Hold the analyzing for later.

5. Once you feel you are pretty solid with the being-in-truth mode, try writing some true statements about the situation in your original question. If possible, keep your emotions calm

and matter of fact, almost like an unbiased newscaster reporting on the situation.

In between the statements about your question, continue to write the easy, obvious statements. These will keep you on the "truth train."

6. Now go back to your original question. Write out the question and then *without thinking*, write an answer. Don't evaluate until you finish writing. Just write whatever comes into your mind after writing the question out.

7. Go back to what you wrote at first and read aloud everything you have written. As you read, notice the tone of your voice and whether it "rings true" or not.

Continue to notice what your voice sounds like as you read the final answer you wrote. Does that feel true to you? It very likely will.

The Truth Train

What makes this exercise so worthwhile is that it is like boarding the "truth train." Once you get on that stream of consciousness, there are many truths that will reveal themselves to you.

Note that the statements don't need to be the grand truth of the universe as a whole, but rather they should be as truthful as your own perceptions allow – the statements are true for you personally, and may not be true for everyone else.

SHORT VERSION – TRUTH-TELLING

1. Write down a question.

2. Begin by writing *easy* true statements.

3. Experiment with making the statements more descriptive.

4. Allow your writing to also include any other thoughts or images that come into your mind (but continue with the easy true statements as well).

5. Try writing some true statements about the situation in your original question in a calm and matter-of-fact way (along with the easy statements). Write like an unbiased newscaster reporting on the situation.

6. Write out the original question and then, without thinking, write an answer.

7. Go back and read aloud everything you have written while noticing the tone of your voice and whether it "rings true" or not.

Reporting an Issue in Nonspecific Language

Have you noticed how a friend who is having a problem often wants to tell you the whole thing with lots and lots of detail? The more details they tell you, the more worked up they get about it. They often want to include the exact wording people said ("And then he said to me... And I said to him...") and then how each person reacted to what was said.

Does the person who is listening really need to know each one of those details? If not, why do people tell it that way?

There could be many reasons. Each person has their own sorts of thought patterns, but one thing that they all have in common is that each time the person gives an exact detail, it makes their story sound more unique and important. This is their own special story – like no other story in the world – and people like a good story!

The reality is that although our life situations *are* important to *us*, the human experience has been going on for thousands of years. Human beings have been experiencing heartbreak, grief, shocking change, success, surprises, revelations...

As one playwright pointed out, there aren't very many plots in the human story. It's the details that make them interesting. And those details can give us the feeling that we are the only people in history who have ever felt this way. We are so special!

What is the need to feel special? Our primitive brain reads "special" as "important." A person, or animal, who is important *survives*.

The important ones get the best of everything – mates, food, shelter, other people doing their chores... Being special/ important is a basic survival drive.

In our stories about our individual life dramas, those important-making details also bring with them a lot of emotion. Emotions have a way of overriding our logical minds. Things can get blown way out of proportion once our emotions take hold.

One way to circumvent the emotional sting is to generalize the situation. There is something about hearing it in its generalized form that gives our problem-solving mind a chance to come up with solutions or to at least put it into a larger context.

It may feel very important to us, but it will not stop the sun from rising tomorrow. Even for us, it is probably not a life or death situation.

Example: *Helen has a coworker that criticizes her and she gets upset.*

That generalizes to: *Someone criticizes someone. That upsets the person being criticized.*

General statements: *People don't like being criticized. It happens a lot. This is part of being human. Every living person on the earth today and in the past, has also had the experience of being criticized at some point.*

Now that Helen sees it in the larger context, she can begin to work with it in a calmer way. Realizing that this is a universal experience, she could look to see how other people have chosen to handle it. This is something *everyone* has to deal with. Since every single person in her life has dealt with criticism at some point, she has a lot of company.

"I feel your pain."

After having an NDE (near-death experience) where she experienced a loving communion with Jesus, my mother had a vibrant prayer life. She had a list of people's prayer requests and each morning she would go through the list and pray for each of them individually. She said once that her morning prayer time was often the best part of her day.

At one point she hurt her back and needed to lie flat while it healed. What to do with all that time? For some people, when they are experiencing something difficult, it is soothing to have someone say, "I feel your pain." Somehow not being alone in that pain eases it a bit.

So, as she lay there, my mother got the idea that there were probably other people in the world at that very moment who were also flat on their backs with pain.

That pain was probably similar to her own. It was an ideal time to pray for those people. She could do so with a full knowledge of the pain they were feeling because, at that moment, she herself was indeed feeling it, too. So, she spent many hours praying for others as she lay there, knowing how they felt and being with them in her prayerful way.

No matter what difficulty, pain, or sorrow we are feeling, there are always other people right at that same moment somewhere in the world feeling the same way. We are not the only ones.

Explain It to a Child

A friend recently wrote a song. As she was listening to the recording she had made of it, she suddenly realized that a particular phrase sounded very similar to a song written by another person. She reworked that phrase to make it different and made a new recording before submitting it for copyright.

The song was written for a six-year-old in her family. The child had already heard the first version. "What happened to the song? Why did you change it?'

As my friend said to me, "How do you explain copyright laws to a six-year-old?"

Obviously, reciting the law as it reads would not be the thing to do. My friend needed to put it into very simple terms.

"When a person writes a song that is their very own, it has to be new and different. People are not allowed to use parts of other people's songs. Everybody's song has to be different."

Would it help to include the information that during the Baroque Era it was okay to quote parts of other people's music? No, that would just complicate things. When explaining something to a six-year-old, it needs to be in a simplified form that will make sense to them.

Writing out your dilemma in the words that a six-year-old would understand can also make *what is really going on* clearer to yourself.

Storytelling

Another way to get insights into a difficult situation you are facing is to put it into a story that sounds like a fairytale. Here is an example of a story someone told me that explained the coping mechanism he developed to withstand his father's abuse. Sadly, that also caused him a different kind of pain. See if you can understand it all by reading his story.

Once upon a time, there was a little boy named Jimmy. He was a quiet kid, but he liked to play with other kids. As he got to be a little bit older the playing got pretty rough.

The kids were throwing snowballs that were hard when they hit him. The snowballs kept hitting him, coming faster and faster, and it hurt.

So what Jimmy did was he built a wall out of the snow. He could duck behind the wall when the snowballs came at him. He kept building the wall all around on all sides. The bigger and better the wall was, the safer Jimmy was. Soon none of the kids could hurt him.

But there was a big man. The big man was so much bigger than the wall. He reached over the wall and hurt the boy again and again.

There wasn't any way to make the wall high enough to protect the boy from the big man. The boy had to think of something to make the man stop hurting him.

Then he had an idea. He made a big smiling face on the outside of the wall. Everyone just saw a smiling face, so they didn't hurt the boy anymore. But now the boy was all alone inside the wall.

No one came in there and he was always alone.

Writing in the 3ʳᵈ Person

Did you ever notice that when a friend tells you about a problem, all kinds of helpful suggestions occur to you? Maybe you see some easy, effective solutions that your friend hadn't even thought of. Somehow helping someone else sort things out can be so much easier than solving our own dilemmas.

Writing in the 3ʳᵈ person is a helpful way to put ourselves in the easy, creative mode we access when it isn't our own problem. Below is an example of how a woman named Helen might write out her situation in the 3ʳᵈ person.

Example:

Helen is a very nice person. She is kind to people and likes to see other people be happy. She also feels bad when she sees unkindness, especially when it is someone being unkind to herself!

She is having a challenge now with a man named Joe at her job. He makes rude critical remarks about her work and this upsets her. First, she feels hurt and then she feels angry and then she would like to retaliate somehow. Then she feels mad at herself for even thinking how she would like to do something bad to Joe. That's not being kind!

All and all, she ends up feeling upset and she says it just ruins her day. I wonder if Helen should quit her job.

That is probably not the best idea.

Maybe she will come up with another way to handle it. I remember Helen counseling a friend who had a situation like that. Helen told her friend to imagine a big protective bubble around herself before going into work.

Helen said that when her friend had the bubble around her, she wouldn't feel bothered at all. The bubble would be like having sound insulation around herself.

Funny. Helen told her friend to do that, but when it happened to Helen herself, she forgot about it. I think Helen should at least try it.

****

CHAPTER FOUR

Dialogues

Non-dominant Hand, People, and Pets

Dialogues give you different perspectives on your present situation. The ones you dialogue with may not have direct answers for you, but getting their perspectives can loosen things up so that you then come up with solutions you had not thought of before.

Or, of course, they may just give you the answers you need!

Non-dominant Hand*

Use a spiral notebook that opens up flat. Each hand has its own pen/pencil. The left hand writes on the left page and the right hand on the right page.

It can be helpful to give the non-dominant hand a thicker pen, more like what a child might first use when they are learning to write. This part of ourselves will relate more to our child-self.

* The hand that you usually use to write is your **dominant hand** (so your right hand, if you are right-handed). The other hand (your left hand, if you are right-handed) is your **non-dominant hand.**

Start by writing a statement with your dominant hand, then write a response with your non-dominant hand. The dialogue then continues back and forth.

In the example below, the non-dominant hand is writing in CAPITAL LETTERS.

I think Joe at work doesn't like me.

HE'S AN IDIOT.

I'm not sure how to deal with him.

TELL HIM TO GET LOST.   (or something more insulting)

I think that would get me into trouble.

WHO CARES? HE DESERVES IT.

Ha-ha! I can just see his reaction! But really, I can't do that.

WHY NOT?

I'll get fired.

WOULDN'T IT BE WORTH IT? YOU ARE WORTH MORE THAN THAT. GET A BETTER JOB.

Even if I didn't mind getting fired, I don't want to treat people like that. I'd like a better way to handle it. Something that will make me feel good about it. I want to feel like I am powerful.

JUST IGNORE HIM. HE DOESN'T COUNT IN YOUR LIFE.

I wonder if I could do that.

OF COURSE YOU CAN. NO BIG DEAL.

Ha-ha! No big deal. Sounds good (smiles).

Dialogues with Others

Here are some suggestions of others to dialogue with followed by some examples.

- A kind, wise grandparent
- A teacher from your past – school teacher, coach, music teacher, art teacher, swim instructor...
- An author you have read books by
- Someone you have met, heard lecture, or read books by – a spiritual teacher, pastor, priest, rabbi, guru
- Your future self – imagine you are a particular age (in the future) and you are looking back on who you are now
- A superhero or character from a movie, book, or game that you like
- Your favorite comedian, talk show host, podcaster, radio personality, actor or actress
- Abraham Lincoln or other statesmen from the past
- Someone who is successful or at the top of a field that you are interested in (or would like to be working in) – if someone asked you to give an example of a successful person, who would you choose?
- Your dog, cat, horse, or other pet
- Something in nature – a bird, tree, flower, mountain stream, wild animal...
- The person you would be if you were helping a friend...
- See more about spirit guides, your soul, Higher Self and others in Chapter 6.

The basic idea is to choose someone whose opinion you would respect or someone (like a pet) who would see things very differently than you do. You have probably already exhausted your own ideas. Getting some other viewpoints can help you see things in a new and helpful way.

Example #1
A Teacher from Your Past

1. Start by writing a short description of the one you will dialogue with.

Mrs. Johnson was my third-grade teacher. I liked her because she was always fair with everyone. She was also good at explaining things. She would encourage me and show me that it wasn't so hard to do things.

2. Write out what it is that you would like clarity on.

Hi, Mrs. Johnson. It is so good to talk to you again. You are probably in heaven now and can see things in a way that is even wiser than before. I want to thank you for helping me when I was a kid.

I have this problem with a guy named Joe. He works with me at my job and whenever he is around, he makes me feel bad. He makes these remarks about whatever I am doing, like I can't do the job right. But I can! I do a perfectly good job. Probably better than he does! It makes me so angry and spoils my day. I just want to hit him!

3. Put down the pen for a moment and take a deep breath. As you let your breath out remember Mrs. Johnson and imagine that you are now her. If you remember her clothing, imagine you are wearing that clothing.

If you remember any little habit she had – like tilting her head a certain way or pressing her lips together – do that now. You can also have a hat or scarf you put on each time you write as Mrs. Johnson.

If imagining yourself to be her doesn't come easily to you, instead, think she is now on the other end of the telephone and you will write down what you hear her saying.

4. Begin writing using the name that she would call you. *"Hello, Helen..."* If you don't get anything, just make it up. This isn't a test. Pretending is fine. The point is to get benefit from this (not to prove anything to anyone).

SHORT VERSION OF THE STEPS

Example #1: A Teacher from Your Past

1. Start by writing a short description of the one you will dialogue with.

2. Write out what it is that you would like clarity on.

3. Put down the pen for a moment and take a deep breath. As you let your breath out remember the teacher and imagine that you are now her. You can also imagine that she is on the other end of the telephone and you will write down what you hear her saying.

4. Begin writing using the name that she would call you.

If you don't get anything, just make it up. This isn't a test. Pretending is fine. The point is to get benefit from this (not to prove anything to anyone).

Example #2: An Author You Like

1. It may be helpful to first read a few passages from one of their books or to watch a video of the author speaking.

2. Start by writing a short description of the author you will dialogue with.

I started reading Wayne Dyer's books when I was a teenager. I really like him because he had his problems but kept working on them. I could see how he got stronger and wiser with each new book he wrote. And he had a big heart. He really cared about people and wanted to help them. I think if he met me, he would want to help me now.

3. Write out what it is that you would like clarity on. Imagine that it is a letter or email that you would send to him.

Hi, Wayne. You have helped me so much with all your books. I want to thank you from deep in my heart. You were always learning and helping people and even showing us that you were vulnerable, too.

I have this problem with a guy named Joe. He works with me at my job and whenever he is around, he makes me feel bad. He makes these remarks about whatever I am doing, like I can't do the job right. But I can! I do a perfectly good job. Probably better than he does! It makes me so angry and spoils my day.

What do you think I should do?

4. This time try standing up and taking a minute to imagine that you are Wayne Dyer. Think about how he talks.

5. Sit down the way you think he would and (pretending you are Wayne Dyer) read what you have written as though you are Wayne opening a letter or email.

6. You know the way Wayne writes about things because you have read his books. Start writing as though you are Wayne writing a response to your email or letter.

"Well hello, Helen. It's nice to hear from you. I'm glad you liked my books. Which one was your favorite?" ...

SHORT VERSION OF THE STEPS

Example #2: An Author You Like

1. Read a few passages from one of the author's books.

2. Write a short description of the author you will dialogue with.

3. Write out what it is that you would like clarity on as though it is a letter or email you would send to him.

4. Stand up and take a minute to imagine that you are the author. Think about how he talks and acts.

5. Sit down the way you think he would and (pretending you are the author) read what you have written as though you are opening a letter or email.

6. Start writing a response to your email or letter (as though you are the author).

Example #3: Your Pet Dog

You can do this through writing, but if your pet is still alive, you can just talk this over with them and imagine what they might say in response.

If your pet has already passed, then you would write it out in a similar way as you did for the other examples. Below is a dog who has passed on.

1. Start by writing what you particularly appreciated about your pet.

Hi Chow-chow. You know sometimes it feels like you are still here with me. It's just that I can't see you. You always made me feel safe. And I felt loved, too. You were such a wonderful companion. I hope when I die that you will be there waiting for me. Somehow, I think you will be.

Right now, I am having trouble with this guy named Joe. He works with me at my job and whenever he is around, he makes me feel bad. He makes these remarks about whatever I am doing, like I can't do the job right. But I can! I do a perfectly good job. Probably better than he does! It makes me so angry and spoils my day.

What do you think I should do?

2. Imagine yourself stroking your dog's head and feel that reassurance you always felt when he was there with you. He may indeed be there. Many mediums see people's pets with them when they come for a reading. Often the pets (in their animal spirit bodies) will be sitting at their person's feet or curled up next to them.

If you have the feeling your beloved pet is there, they probably are! So greet them and let them know that the bond of love that you two share is still vibrant and alive between you.

3. So now, let's hear what Chow-chow has to say.

"I love you, love you, love you. I am always here with you. I love it best when you are happy and you laugh with me as I jump in the air! That man at work probably has a crush on you and wants your attention. Just like when you would talk on the phone and I wanted you to play with ME! He probably doesn't know how to get you to like him, so he just does whatever he can to get your attention. Why wouldn't he? You are the MOST WONDERFUL PERSON and everyone would want to be with you and have your attention all the time!

So now, that gives you another perspective!

SHORT VERSION OF THE STEPS

Example #3: Your Pet Dog

1. If your pet is still alive, you can just talk this over with them and imagine what they might say in response.

If your pet has passed, then you would write it out in a similar way as you did for the other examples.

2. Write what you particularly appreciated about your pet, and then explain what the present problem is.

3. Imagine yourself stroking your pet and feel the reassurance you always felt when he was there with you. Let him know that the bond of love that you two share is still vibrant and alive between you.

4. Write out your pet's response.

CHAPTER FIVE

Who and What?

Is It Useful?

There are multiple helpful ones in the spirit world who would be delighted to interact with you in a beneficial way. Your own openness to what you would like to receive is like dialing up a particular level of helpers.

If you want a guide who is very advanced, they probably will not be as helpful with nitty-gritty things in your daily life. However, there are others who are closer to the "earth realm" who are also ready and willing to help.

Worlds Within Worlds

As I sit here writing this book, there are many different types of information present here in this room that I cannot see. Here is a brief list of those broadcasts.

- 20-25 AM radio stations
- 20-25 FM radio stations
- Wifi signals from my own modem and from my neighbors
- Cellular phone signals – at least 3 providers
- Cordless phone signal
- GPS signals

I can't see any of those signals myself. If I do not have a device – radio, phone, etc. – I do not know if those signals are operating or not.

Modern science tells us that although we perceive ourselves as solid beings, that we are actually not solid at all. What we think of as our bodies is mostly space. Strange to think that all those signals listed above are also moving through my body at this very moment and will continue to do that 24/7 unless a universal power outage shuts them all down.

Describing to someone in 1776 about how the spirit world is actually right here right now, in our very midst, would be much more difficult than explaining it today. We now accept that there is a lot going on that our physical receptors (sight, hearing, touch, smell, and taste) do not access.

What is called a "sixth sense" is the ability to pick up on some of the additional information here that our basic five senses don't perceive.

Our brains are constantly sifting through all the information that is continually coming to us through multiple avenues. This sorting out process cuts out a lot of what we *could* potentially have awareness of.

If we begin to give priority and importance to things like the "still, small voice" (page 36), our awareness of that will increase because those "signals" will not be filtered out as much.

In earlier times, people thought of heaven as being up in the sky, somewhere far away. Now we are realizing that it is all here in the same "space." There is nowhere else. However, just as the different stations on the radio each speak or sing in their own frequency, the different "worlds" also each have their own integrity and uniqueness.

When we open ourselves to a wider experience of reality, it is possible to pick up on some of the frequencies that are not what we call the "physical world."

One could argue that what appears to us as nonphysical actually is physical, too, even though it is not perceived as so by our five senses. That discussion is not pertinent to this book. What *is* pertinent here is that **there is much that is indeed real even though it is not physically apparent to us.**

Humanity has been aware of this "other world" for longer than recorded history. That other-world awareness has given rise to all sorts of religions and belief systems about what those worlds are, who or what is a part of them, and how those worlds interface with us as we have our physical experience here.

The aim of this book is not to prove anything about who or what those worlds are, but rather to give you some tools to access some of the help and wisdom that is available to all of us by increasing our abilities to receive the helpful communications and gifts that can come to us from those realms.

Wider Reality

To simplify the writing here, anything which is not part of the known physical world (what our five senses perceive) will be referred to as the **wider reality**. Please substitute any other term that you prefer. Some other ways to express it might be: *spirit world, nonphysical world, spiritual realms, greater world, the great unknown, heavenly realms,* or *other levels of consciousness.*

Some of the multitude of options of who and what is available to us in the *wider reality* will be listed later in this chapter.

Not about WHO,
but rather, WHAT

If you were in a new town and looking for a particular restaurant, how would you find it?

Let's imagine your GPS tells you that you have arrived at the location, but you don't see the restaurant. You see someone walking by and ask them if they know where that restaurant is. They tell you it is two doors down. You walk there and find the restaurant just where they said it would be.

Does it matter to you whether the person who gave you the information was male or female? Would their age, how they were dressed, or the color of their hair make a difference?

No. You wanted some specific information, and you got it. That is what matters.

Now it could also be that there were five people around when you couldn't see the restaurant. In that case, you probably made an evaluation about which of those five people would be most likely to give you the correct information.

Let's imagine one of those five people was a famous person, one of your sports heroes, favorite musicians, or a famous actor. You are thrilled to have the opportunity to have contact with them. You have your photo taken with them and then ask if they know where the restaurant is. They say it is closed.

But that isn't actually true. The restaurant is open and just two doors down.

In the same way as the person looking for the restaurant, when we are asking for helpful information from the *wider reality*, the smart thing is to keep the focus on our true goal – **helpful information**.

You may have heard that someone has access to Mary, the Blessed Mother. That may or may not be true. If you hear what the Blessed Mother is supposed to have said, do you assume that it *must* be true because she said it? If you do, it would be like the person in the story who gets the wrong answer from the famous person.

Whatever information is received should be evaluated on its own merit, not because someone else believes (or you yourself believe) the information is from a particular person, angel, master, or guide.

In Chapter 4 you may have chosen to do a dialogue with Abraham Lincoln. Was it *really* Abraham Lincoln that reminded you of something that helped you get clarity?

Maybe yes, maybe no. But that is not the important thing. It could be that imagining what he might say to you was the vehicle that brought you to the destination you were seeking. Great! No need to prove it one way or the other. That is not the point.

If you find your mind beginning to ponder, "Was it *really* Abraham Lincoln? That can be playing into the ego's desire to feel important (important enough that Lincoln would take some time to talk to you). Thoughts like that are likely to sabotage the benefits that are there for you to receive.

So, to get clear guidance about a particular question or decision in your life, it is not important *who* you got it from, but rather **was it correct, was it true?** That should be how you judge its value. We'll explore more about how to evaluate the information you get in the last chapter in this book.

The Phone Line is Love

Going back to the restaurant story, if there were five people there, you would have a choice of who to ask. You would then evaluate which person you thought might most likely give you the right information and maybe also who might be most pleasant to talk to.

Likewise, it is worthwhile to discern which of the many options in the *wider reality* is most likely to give you the help you need in the way you would like it.

No matter who or what you communicate with in the *wider reality*, the connecting "phone line" should be love. If it does not feel like love to you, drop that communication line and go elsewhere.

The spiritual law is that you have the right to reject or excuse anyone or anything that does not feel good to you. You are in charge of your own experience. You are the one to determine if you interact or not.

If there is a feeling of being criticized, manipulated, or scared, those are not the helpful ones you want to deal with. If it begins to feel that way at any point, simply say, "Not interested. Leave." One way to test them is to say, "Let me feel your love." If you don't get a wonderful, peaceful embrace, reject them.

Remember, there are so many others that are ready and waiting to be of the greatest help to you. There is no need to settle for anything less. Not 80% or 90% good. Only go with something that feels 100% good to you.

The criteria I use is that they must be loving, wise, and helpful. All three. Why focus on anything less?

It Goes Both Ways

Likewise, if you try to manipulate, overpower or push the helpers in the *wider reality*, they will simply disappear. You can certainly challenge what they say – no problem with that, and doing that is quite useful – but if you try to take control over them, the line of communication will end. They are never intimidated and are not obligated to stick around.

The help they give us goes beyond what we ourselves can do. This is a precious gift. It is best to treat it as such.

Joy, Laughter

Note that there is no need to be serious or sanctimonious about the whole interaction. On the contrary, there is often a good deal of humor and laughter in these relationships. The joy of those in the *wider reality* is infectious and a pure delight! A lighthearted feeling brings you even closer to them. They love it when we laugh with delight!

Happy Memories

With family and friends in the spirit world that you want to connect with, thinking of the happy times you shared with them and feeling that inner smile and glow as you remember them, is an excellent way to connect.

Thinking about your own pain in missing them is like a thick fog that makes it hard for them to get through to you. This is one reason the deceased loved ones come to people while they are sleeping (it wasn't "just a dream"). When your thoughts and sadness are not interfering with the communications, it is easier for the spirit people to connect with you.

Some of the Many Helpful Options
in the Wider Reality

Here are some suggestions of people or beings in the *wider reality* that you might want to open yourself to. It is a busy place!

Loved Ones in Spirit

Everyone has family members and friends who have passed on into the Spirit World. You may not have known your grandparents or great-grandparents, but that doesn't mean they aren't aware of you!

If you have children of your own, don't you think you will continue to be interested in their lives after you pass out of your physical body? No one got here without having parents. You may not have grown up knowing who they were, but they are still connected to you.

You may also have friends, other family members, or pets who are now in spirit. Not everyone in spirit is easy to contact, but you can ask to connect with them, and it is very likely that you will. A good way to start is by remembering a warm and happy time with them. The phone line is love. When you feel the love you have for them, it is like dialing them up and giving them a call.

Religious Figures

Jesus, Mother Mary, John the Divine, and other religious figures are here in the ethers awaiting your calls to them. Some people have specific prayers that help them feel the connection more clearly. Others have pictures, rosaries, or other religious objects that help them connect.

These connections are a personal experience that we each have with these powerfully loving divine beings. No other person here can give you that or take it away from you.

Remember that the important thing is how the connection with them affects you. There is no need to prove to someone else afterwards who it is you connected with. All that matters is what your own experience was and the benefits it brought you.

Some others you can connect with:

- Saint Germain, Saint Francis, Saint Brigid, Saint Anthony, Saint Anne, and other saints
- Mary Magdalene
- Buddha/Siddhartha
- Quan Yin
- Goddess Sekhmet, Goddess Isis, other Egyptian deities
- Lord Krishna, Kali
- Norse Gods and Goddesses
- God Pan

Angels

- Archangel Michael, Archangel Raphael, other angels and archangels
- Your own guardian angels (people often have two)

Spiritual Teachers & Guides

See more about the teachers and guides in Chapter 6.

- Monks/Nuns from different religious orders
- Lao Tzu, Confucius
- Djwal Khul (D.K.), Tibetan Masters
- Koot Hoomi
- Power animals
- A guru you have a relationship with

Historical Figures

The writings of the author Frank DeMarco (not the cinematographer) are a good example of a person making connections with a number of different people in the *wider reality*. You can read DeMarco's conversations with Ernest Hemingway, Carl Jung, and others on his blog (ofmyownknowledge.com) and in his many books.

Suggestions:

- George Washington, Thomas Jefferson, Benjamin Franklin, Abraham Lincoln, Susan B. Anthony
- Galileo, Nicola Tesla, Albert Einstein
- Leonardo da Vinci, Michelangelo
- Plato, Aristotle, Socrates, Descartes
- Madame Curie
- Napoleon, Alexander the Great
- Cleopatra, Hatshepsut, Nefertiti
- Beethoven, Franz Liszt, Clara Schumann
- William Shakespeare, Charles Dickens, Tolstoy, George Eliot, Anne Frank
- Amelia Earhart
- Joan of Arc
- Rosa Parks, Harriet Tubman
- kings, queens, other royalty

More Recent Famous People

- Michael Jackson
- Marilyn Monroe
- Elvis
- Princess Diana
- Ruth Bader Ginsberg
- John Lennon
- Steve Jobs
- Maya Angelou
- Anthony Bourdain
- Nelson Mandela

Spiritual Authors, Motivational Speakers
(both living now or in Spirit)

- Alice Bailey
- Edgar Cayce
- Robert Monroe
- Wayne Dyer
- Louise Hay

- Tony Robbins
- Ester Hicks
- Paul Selig
- Joe Dispenza
- Greg Braden

Technical Experts in Your Profession

A good example of this is documented in the book, *Ears of the Angels*, by Deena Zalkind Spear. She is a violin maker and acoustical researcher who developed relationships with a number of the best violin makers of the past (begin reading about that on page 33).

Nature Spirits

- Fairies, Fauns, Water Sprites, and other nature spirits

Are fairies real or just the stuff of children's fairytales? There are some people who are blessed with what is often referred to as "2nd sight." They claim to both see the fairies and to even interact with them. An example is the book, *The Real World of the Fairies* by Dora Kunz (she is also the founder of Therapeutic Touch).

In *The Occult Diaries of R Ogilvie Crombie*, Robert Ogilvie Crombie (known as "ROC" from the Findhorn Community) wrote about his experience with a faun who was dancing around the trees in a park. This led to a series of relationships with other nature spirits and eventually their god Pan.

Species Devas

Another member of the early Findhorn Community, Dorothy Maclean, became aware of the "devas" of different plant species. These are the over-lighting intelligences of each of the species in our gardens and the rest of nature.

For example, you might feel an affinity with a tree near where you live. When you sit under it, you get a particular feeling. It's a feeling you don't get anywhere else. You may even talk to that tree and get some sort of response.

Your tree is unique. There is no other tree in the world exactly like it. However, if it is an oak tree, it is included in the devic intelligence which encompasses all the oak trees.

Making a relationship with your particular oak tree also connects you with the *oak-tree deva*. You may move somewhere else and find another oak tree to commune with. That tree will be different, but there will also be a sameness to it that you can recognize.

When your oak tree dies, the *oak-tree deva* will live on and be manifested in other oak trees. You can read more about the devas in *The Findhorn Garden* by the Findhorn Community. Dorothy Maclean has also authored a number of books.

There is a similar idea in Native American traditions. "Grandfather Eagle" is not one particular eagle, but rather the deva of all eagles. "Eagle" may manifest as an actual eagle that you see around you. That eagle may interact with you as a representative of Eagle, but when that particular eagle dies, Grandfather Eagle will continue to live.

There is much we can learn from the devas of the plants, animals, trees, birds, insects, rocks, crystals, and more. Dora Kunz told me that each piece of property or location also has what she called an "over-lighting angel" with whom we can relate.

Your Own Past-Lives or Future Lives

You may have done a past-life regression or had a spontaneous memory of having lived as a different person in another place and time.

It is possible to have a relationship with this other part of yourself. That other "self" has had different life experiences, lived in a different culture, and will see things in different ways. Learning about that can be helpful.

Something that people often find with this is, although the circumstances are very different, there tend to be certain themes that repeat. It can be seen as different chapters in a book where the main character (you) learns certain life lessons.

For example, if the subject was learning about familial relationships – families – the person experiences being mother, father, daughter, son, oldest child, youngest child, middle child, grandparent, childless aunt or uncle...

If the subject of the book was learning about romantic relationships, in the various lifetimes/chapters the person would also find themselves in different roles – the one who rejects a lover, the lover who is rejected, the one who loves even when it is difficult, the one who avoids love all together...

If in your present life you are having a lot of trouble coming to terms with having been rejected by a lover, connecting with a lifetime where you were the one who did the rejecting could loosen up your feeling about your present situation.

You are not just the rejected one. You are both. It happened both ways. Each person always has their reasons and each person plays a role in the events that take place.

****

CHAPTER SIX

Inspired Writing

Your Wise Self, Higher Self, Soul, Spirit Guides, Ecstatic Poetry and Trance Mediums

Hopefully, you have now done some imagined dialogues with those in the *wider reality*. In this chapter, we'll take it a bit further into what could open the door to authentic interactions with those helpful ones who are awaiting our requests (that may well have already started happening for you!). A good way to begin to attune yourself with these "higher vibrations" is to first spend some time with the aspects of yourself that are closer to these wonderful, helpful beings.

Note: The terms used in this chapter are not definitive but rather an attempt to describe possible **avenues of connection**. Of course, please substitute any terms you prefer. Here are some basic definitions of how these terms will be used.

Wise Self = when you are in a clear, centered state-of-being without the fog of emotions clouding your ability to see things simply *as they are* (rather than through a lens of emotional assumptions and projections).

Higher Self = this is an aspect of you that sees things – your life and what goes on there with yourself and other people – from a higher, broader perspective. It is also closer to the spiritual realms and is more attuned to how those in the higher realms see things.

Your Soul = the ongoing aspect of yourself that will continue on after your physical body dies.

Your Wise Self

Your Wise Self is loving and wise and doesn't get carried away with emotional states. One way to tap into this part of yourself is to do the Truth-Telling exercise (page 42). Things are what they are. Your Wise Self does not need to embellish things or react to how wrong you may think things are.

For example, maybe you just lost your job. Your mind is churning with how unjustly you feel you were treated. Your mind searches for someone to blame. "If-only" thoughts about how it could have ended differently come into your mind. You may find yourself snapping at people around you or clenching your teeth. The prominent thoughts in your mind are all about how *wrong* it all is. "This should not have happened. It shouldn't be this way."

After you have been experiencing those emotions for a while, you may want to get out of it (that way of feeling). The truth-telling exercise can be a real lifesaver in times like this because it reconnects you with your Wise Self.

Your Wise Self has compassion for the emotional tumult you are feeling, but there isn't the constant attempt to make things different than they are or to blame someone else (or yourself) for what has happened.

You are where you are right now. That's all. Tomorrow you will either move on to other things or hold on to the emotions you are presently feeling. No judgment there. That is simply true. You can stay wrought up as long as it feels important to you to do that. After all, experiencing all these emotions is part of the human-life experience.

When you have had enough of the emotional wild ride, your Wise Self will be helpful in finding solutions to your present situation and giving you positive ideas about moving forward.

1. After doing the truth-telling exercise, write out how you see your *present-moment* situation. Don't write about the job or how you got let go. That is all from the past. Make true statements about you and your situation as it is *now*.

2. Begin to include possible-optional-futures in your statements. That might include collecting unemployment for a while, starting your own business, taking a live-in position with someone who needs help, moving to a different area, or getting a job that suits you better. Let your mind begin to grasp that this could be the beginning of a big improvement in your life.

3. Let your Wise Self come up with a version of your life one year in the future where things have worked out in a way that is even better for you. The truth is that there are multiple – uncountable, there so many – options that could potentially be your future. Whatever you write about now does not need to be something that you then set your hopes on. It is just to introduce your mind to the idea that there are many, many future options.

4. If you write four more possible futures, that's even better (a total of five). Make the last one a silly fantasy. It doesn't need to be logical at all. It's just about realizing that life goes on. All is not lost. You have options.

5. Write down any additional messages your Wise Self has for you right now.

Your Higher Self

The following exercise is a way to begin to distinguish the perspective of your Higher Self. Interestingly enough, it is called that because it literally feels as though you are above things and looking down on it all.

With the invention of drones, and their wide availability, we get these higher perspectives on things much more often now. Think about how differently people saw the world before air travel. A person's ideas about things would have been much smaller – often all they saw was their own families, villages and towns. Many people lived their whole lives within a very small area (by our standards).

Doing the *Reporting an Issue in Nonspecific Language* exercise (page 48) may have begun to attune you to this higher, wider perspective on things. Those in the *wider reality* are not as limited with time and space as we are.

Example: *Someone cut a man off in traffic. "What are they doing?!! What an idiot!!" He's all riled up. As he continues driving, it is all he can think about. Suddenly, he gets a call from his wife. Her voice sounds strange. She asks him to please come home immediately and then she hangs up.*

Luckily, he is just a few minutes from home. When he walks in he sees his wife has been crying. She tells him she has been diagnosed with a terminal disease and has just 3-4 weeks left to live. How important is the idiot who cut him off in traffic right now? Not at all.

Shocking experiences like this tend to put everything in our lives into a different context. This is like the difference between the everyday-self's perspective on things and the Higher Self's perspective.

One way to jog yourself out of a small-minded reaction to an event is to ask yourself, "If I found out I had only two months left to live, how important would this be?

Another way is to literally **lift up your perspective**. You can also do this exercise by drawing it, instead of writing it out.

Example: Think of something fairly recent where you had an interaction with another person.

1. Write a 1-2 sentence description of what happened as far as you remember it.

2. Now imagine you were hovering just above the two of you and could "see" the thoughts going on between you. Whatever sorts of impressions come to you are fine. You may see colors, streaks, thoughts that weren't even spoken... You can even make the words the two people are speaking like callout bubbles in cartoons.

3. Now move up higher. If the two people are in a room, look down on them from the ceiling. If they are outdoors, move to a place that is up about 20 feet above them. What are you seeing now?

4. Next move even higher. It is like being a drone that is looking down on it all. What is your feeling about the whole interaction now? Describe it again.

5. Move even higher. It is like moving out on Google Earth where you can see the whole earth at once. Describe the interaction of the two people from that perspective.

6. You can even take it one step further if you would like. There are a lot of angels and higher beings up there with you now. Discuss with them about the two people's interaction.

Your Soul

Here, the word *soul* is referring to the aspect of yourself that will continue on after your physical body dies.

1. Begin by thinking about what makes your soul different than your everyday personality-self. Does your soul have the same desires as you do? How is the soul's perspective the same or different?

One spiritual teacher I spoke with was sure that our souls have very different agendas than we people do. She emphasized that what our souls care about is "soul-growth," and that this can be difficult for us as people.

Soul growth might come from withstanding a difficult situation or a disability or dramatic event. Not something we would want to go through or ever choose to experience if we had a choice. But the soul, knowing that we survive it all and will not ultimately be harmed by anything that might happen to us here, doesn't mind these situations at all. The challenges are opportunities for soul-growth, so the soul is pleased when they occur.

Another spiritual teacher sees our souls as the part of us that is forever holding us in tenderness. It honors our desires while we are here, and is always attempting to ease things along for us in a most loving way.

Some people describe our souls as each of us having a piece of God in us, so it is the place where we most readily feel connected to the Divine.

What is your view of your soul? One thing most would agree on is that our souls have a wider perspective on things than our everyday personalities do.

Maybe you don't really know who or what your soul is or maybe haven't discovered yet that you will continue after this physical life. That's okay, too. For this exercise, just write a script of what your soul (if you had one) could possibly be and try it out. If something comes of it, that is all for the better. In the end, the definitions don't matter so much, so long as there is benefit.

However, having your script of what you imagine your soul *could* be, will prime the pump for making a connection which can bring you some benefit here. Remember, you don't need to prove anything to anyone else to do this. This is for your benefit!

2. Introduce yourself. Your soul actually knows you better than you know yourself, but in this case, stating the images that you hold of *who you think you are* will make it easier to have a common language, a language that makes sense to you.

For example, if you think of yourself as basically a kind person, your soul can use that as a jumping-off place to teach you about kindness to others and to yourself.

If you say that you are a highly creative person, your soul can relate the lessons of your life to creativity and how that brings benefit to yourself and others. The soul might encourage you to act in creative ways to challenging situations and keep reminding you that because you are so creative, you will be able to come up with completely new ways to deal with things.

Example:

I am a kind person. I like to help people when I can, and I don't want anyone to suffer. Sometimes, though, people just wear me out and I just want to be alone. Some people are so cruel and stupid and other people complain all the time. I wish everyone else would just be kind, too.

3. Next, write out a basic issue that you would like some help with. Example:

I am being challenged at work. A coworker is constantly putting me down. How should I deal with this?

4. Put your pen down and take some time to get still within yourself. You may also want to close your eyes. Begin to notice your breath and how your body is breathing easily and rhythmically. Affirm your openness to being helped by your soul. It can just be a statement or a prayer that is suited to you and your beliefs. Then count your breaths from one to ten.

5. Your prayer has been heard. Even if you do not think of it as a prayer, when you reach out and open yourself by asking for help, it will be received as a prayer.

Let yourself become aware of the love that is present in this moment. Many people will feel it in their hearts. Wherever you feel it is perfect for you. You may have a body sensation that goes along with that (like an expanding in your chest) or an image (like a warm glow).

6. Let the love-feeling expand down your arm and pick up the pen. Begin to write.

If nothing comes right away, begin with, "Dear beloved one, I hear your distress about..."

Example: *Dear beloved one, I hear your distress about this man at your work. You are a kind person and you would like others to be kind as well. Everyone treating each other with kindness would be so sweet and beautiful.*

There are two things that are perhaps a bit hard to understand and do here, but I will share them with you and hope that is helpful.

This man is not being kind to you, and you feel he ought to be kind. This puts you into a conflict with him.

When there is conflict there will also be distress. This distress is unpleasant and hard to deal with.

One way for you to start feeling better is to cease with wanting him to be different than he is. Each person has their reasons for their behaviors. You do not know what is behind his actions.

He may have a very, very difficult home life. It makes him so angry that he would like to scream and yell and beat someone with his fist. He tries not to harm others in those ways.

So, he lowers his violent reactions to the abuse he suffers, but he isn't able to transform himself completely. What is left from the anger he feels inside at being treated so poorly at home comes out in smaller ways at work.

It is not actually something he does to hurt you personally, but he has so much painful anger, that just making his rude remarks is the best he can do.

If someday you are able to hold him in compassion for his situation, that will actually change the dynamic between the two of you. Instead of finding fault with him for his actions, you may be able to see that, like yourself, he is doing his best.

Your gift of kindness to him – in not holding him in anger for his actions – can help to soothe some of the pain he is in.

Being able to soothe another's pain will give you a sense of deep peace and fulfillment for it embodies the beauty and strength that you are. You will feel your own kindness in a deeper and more wonderful way.

7. You will probably sense when there is a completion for that day's dialogue. A good way to end is by thanking your soul for the love and wisdom that has been expressed.

Some people like to read over what was written right away and others like to save it to read a bit later.

SHORT VERSION – YOUR SOUL

For this exercise, *soul* = the aspect of yourself that will continue on after your physical body dies.

1. What is your view of your soul? Begin by thinking about what makes your soul different than your everyday personality-self. Does your soul have the same desires as you do? How is your soul's perspective the same or different?

2. Introduce yourself. Your soul actually knows you better than you know yourself, but in this case, stating the images that you hold of *who you think you are* will make it easier to have a common language, a language that makes sense to you.

3. Write out a basic issue that you would like some help with.

4. Put your pen down and take some time to get still within yourself. You may also want to close your eyes. Begin to notice your breath and how your body is breathing easily and rhythmically. Affirm your openness to being helped by your soul. Then count your breaths from one to ten.

5. Let yourself become aware of the love that is present in this moment.

6. Let the love-feeling expand down your arm and pick up the pen. Begin to write. If nothing comes right away, begin with, "Dear beloved one, I hear your distress about..."

7. A good way to end is by thanking your soul for the love and wisdom that has been expressed. You can read what you have written immediately or wait and read it a bit later.

Spiritual Teachers and Guides

In the early 20th century, the works of Alice Bailey's communications with an *expanded reality* Tibetan master, Djwal Khul, were published. From 1963-1984 the *Seth Material* came through Jane Roberts. More recently, there are channeling books and videos by Ester Hicks, Lee Carroll, Paul Selig, and many others.

There are examples below of some of those teachers you can connect with. Note that no one in the *wider reality* is exclusively connected with any person. These guides do not belong to anyone.

D.K.

I had a funny experience with the Tibetan master/teacher D.K. (Djwal Khul). I was having a cranial sacral session, and as I lay on the massage table I became aware of a spirit-person up in the air above me who was laughing and laughing. It looked something like the statues of the Laughing Buddha. I thought maybe he was Chinese.

His laughter was so contagious that it got to the point where I could not contain it anymore, and I was just laughing out loud. The massage therapist caught it, too. She was laughing now and asked what was going on?

I told her about the spirit person who was so funny and making me laugh so much. She asked, "What's his name?"

When he responded, "Djwal Khul," I thought, "Oh, no! That can't be right. That's Alice Bailey's guide."

He just gave me a look. These teachers are so powerful, they often don't even need words. It was so obvious. Jesus can come to anyone. Why shouldn't Djwal Khul be able to do that, too?

It was a clear teaching to me. No person "owns" any spiritual teacher or guide from the *wider reality*.

Connecting with a Spirit Guide

Suggestions:

- Monks/Nuns from different religious orders
- Lao Tzu, Confucius
- Djwal Khul (D.K.), Tibetan Masters
- Koot Hoomi
- Native American/First Nation people
- Power animals
- A guru you have a relationship with

1. Start by writing a short description of what you imagine one of your spirit guides might be like. Would he/she be a Tibetan Master, a Native American, an African woman shaman, an Obi-Wan Kenobi character, Gandalf from the Hobbit, a wizard, a goddess? If you could choose, what would be your favorite? You may actually already subconsciously sense your guides. This could be why you find certain movie or book characters attractive.

It is also worthwhile asking yourself (and answering) this question because the reality is that our spirit guides can morph into many different forms. Their principal desire is to be in relationship with us. If we want them to be a wise wizard, they will most likely be more than happy to oblige.

I witnessed this in a reading I was doing for a woman who said she wanted to get in touch with one of her guides. I saw a male Native American guide appear next to her when she said that.

At that time, I was using a basket of animal figurines to assist people with making their connections.

The guide reached over her shoulder and positioned a howling wolf figurine so that it was on the top of the ones she was to choose from.

The woman chose the wolf just as the guide had hoped. When I asked her how she felt about wolves, the woman spoke about the wolf referring to it as "she." As she talked, it became obvious that she wanted her guide to be female.

What did the guide do? He switched his vibration and made himself female. The woman was then able to attune herself to him (now her), and was very pleased to begin their relationship.

One way to think of it is that if a spirit guide has had many lifetimes on earth, there would be many different forms they could take. All of that is for another book, but for now, suffice it to say that it is worthwhile for you to make it known what kind of a guide you would like to have.

Making these relationships is about harmonizing vibrations, and it is easier to harmonize with both the people and guides we like better.

Also note that there are multiple helpful ones in the spirit world who would be delighted to interact with you in a beneficial way. Your own openness to what you would like to receive will be like dialing up a particular level of helpers.

As mentioned before, a very advanced guide will not be as helpful with nitty-gritty things in your daily life. However, there are others who are closer to the "earth realm" who are also ready and willing to help.

For example, a friend of mine called on the spirit world to help her find a new car. A man in spirit who had been a car salesman volunteered to help her. He found just the right car and told her where to find it. She went where he said it would be and there it was, just exactly what she needed!

A high-level spiritually advanced guide would not have been the one to ask for that help.

After you have written out what you imagine your guide might be like, be sure to include *the feeling* that you would expect to get from them. My criteria are that anyone I deal with from the *wider reality* must be loving, wise, and helpful.

That is a good place to start, but you might also want to specify that they be gentle with you or that they be very direct in their suggestions (not oblique or metaphoric). That's up to you. But making your desires known is helpful to the guides.

If you don't care about what form the guide presents himself/herself in, skip that part of the description and just write out the *qualities* of the help you are seeking.

2. Write out your question as clearly as you can. Don't try to outguess what language the guides would expect your question to be in. They work on the vibration of truth and love.

Say what you *really* mean. Use the words that you would use in your own head. Be unaffected, honest, and sincere. You don't get extra points for saying you want the best for everyone concerned if you don't actually feel that way in your heart.

Start with where you *are*, not where you think you ought to be. Tell it like it is for you in this moment.

3. In the same way as you did with your soul, make a prayer or affirming statement about your openness to receiving higher guidance.

4. Affirm and commit that you will acknowledge and write down the next impression that comes to you after you take three deep breaths.

5. Breathing in through your nose, take a deep breath from way down in your belly. Breathe out through your mouth blowing slowly like you are creating a gentle breeze.

Do that two more times. On the third breath, as you blow out, notice the next impression that comes to you. It may be a word, an image, a feeling in your body, an emotion... whatever it is, write that down.

6. Continue writing in a similar way as you did in the *Stream of Consciousness* exercise – writing down each word, image, or any other impressions that come to you.

Don't worry if it does not seem to make much sense at the beginning. When you buy a new printer, the first thing that gets printed out is a test page. It's a way to test if the messages being sent to the printer are being processed correctly.

Likewise, the first things you write down may well be like that test page. They are simply a way of checking to see if you are able to perceive the impressions the guide is relaying to you.

If you have a flow established but then things seem to stall, do the three breaths again. *Remember, you are not to analyze or evaluate as you are writing.* That is only to be done afterwards.

7. Once you have established a connection with a guide, you can dialogue in the same way as you did with your soul. Continue with the writing until it feels complete.

8. Be sure to thank the guide at the end. Your appreciation and gratitude will reinforce the bond that is being created between the two of you.

9. Read it over, evaluating what you want to take from it, and make some notes about the important parts.

RECORDING

If it is working well and coming too quickly, try recording it and transcribing it afterwards. If you have a mobile phone, they all have a recording app preinstalled.

SHORT VERSION

CONNECTING WITH A SPIRIT GUIDE

1. Write a short description of what you imagine one of your spirit guides might be like. Be sure to include the feeling that you would expect to get from them. If you don't care about what form the guide presents himself/herself in, skip that part of the description and just write out the *qualities* of the help you are seeking. My criteria are that anyone I deal with from the *wider reality* must be loving, wise, and helpful.

Your own openness to what you would like to receive will be like dialing up a particular level of helpers.

2. Write out your question as clearly as you can. Be honest with where you are in the moment. Use the words that you use in your own head when you think about it.

3. In the same way as you did with your "soul," make a prayer or affirming statement about your openness to receiving higher guidance.

4. Affirm and commit that you will acknowledge and write down the next impression that comes to you after you take three deep breaths.

5. Breathing in through your nose, take a deep breath from way down in your belly. Breathe out through your mouth blowing slowly like you are creating a gentle breeze.

Do that two more times. On the third breath, as you blow out, notice the next impression that comes to you and write that down.

6. Continue writing in a similar way as you did in the *Stream of Consciousness* exercise – writing down each word, image or any other impressions that come to you. It may be like the test page on a new printer at first.

If you have a flow established but then things seem to stall, do the three breaths again.

Remember, you are not to analyze or evaluate as you are writing. That is only to be done afterwards.

7. Once you have established a connection with a guide, you can dialogue in the same way as you did with your soul. Continue with the writing until it feels complete.

8. Thank the guide at the end.

9. Read it over, evaluating what you want to take from it, and make some notes about the important parts.

Follow-up Questions

Many of the dialogue examples only included the beginnings of the dialogues. Once a flow gets established, it can go back and forth the way it did in the *Non-Dominant Hand* dialogue (page 55).

Throughout the dialogue, it is important to be honest and forthright about what you think and feel.

People who were born with psychic-sight have told me that ever since they were children, when someone told a lie, they would see little hook-like forms all around the person's head. If the child asked why the person was lying, people would usually deny it. So they began to realize that other people didn't know about the hooks. The children knew, but the liars didn't realize how easy it was for the children to see they were lying.

Think of the spirit guides as having that ability, too. They know if you are telling the truth, probably even more than you do yourself! Don't try to be any different than you truly are.

If the spirit guide says something that you don't agree with, don't hold back. They don't mind being challenged.

In fact, challenging what they say, is beneficial to both of you. You will get more clarity by challenging them, and they will learn how to communicate with you in a better, more effective way.

For example, if a spirit guide says that it would benefit you to hold someone in compassion and you don't feel like you can do that at all, you can say so.

Example:

I just don't see how that could ever happen. He is a terrible, evil, awful person. He doesn't deserve compassion.

Good. This is expressing how you truly feel. That is your present truth. Now it is up to the guide to see if he/she can expand your view of your own capabilities when it comes to compassion for others. The dialogue continues below with the spirit guide's response.

Having compassion for someone can seem absolutely impossible sometimes. Life can be so hard, and you need to protect yourself. Do you sometimes think that if you got to choose how things in the world would be, that things would be very different?

Yes, I'd like a lot of things to be different.

Like what?

That the evil people like that man never existed at all. He would not even be a part of this world.

What would the world be like then?

It would all be peaceful. People would just be nice to each other. It would be just nice all the time.

And you would like that?

Of course!

Really?

Why wouldn't I?

What kind of movies do you like to see?

I like the ones where someone overcomes a difficulty. They had a problem and then they found a way to make things all work out.

Would you like a movie where things were only peaceful? No bad people or difficulties?

Ohhh... I am beginning to get your point. So okay, it's alright to have some difficulties that we get to overcome, but do I have to have compassion for the bad people?

What do you think?

I suppose I could or I couldn't. The bad people would be there either way.

(waiting)

And, I suppose then that whether I have compassion or not really only matters to me, not what is going on with the other people at all.

(continues to lovingly wait)

So if I can be compassionate or not, that just makes a difference to how I feel.

Yes...

So I can choose it either way – one way feels angry and the other way is peaceful. I'll have to think about that. I think that is enough for me for one day. I need to think this over.

I am delighted to be of service. You are continually held in love and admiration for your courage and fortitude as you move through your life. Call on me whenever you would like and I will be here with you again. I love you.

Thank you.

Accessing Teachings, Knowledge, Philosophies and Understandings

The more you work with the different writing tools, the easier it will be to get direct, clear guidance for anything that is going on in your life. Each one of the exercises creates a vessel into which members of the *wider reality* can insert their influence and eventually their direct expression.

Once communications have been established, rather than asking questions, you can also simply ask what they would like to communicate to you that day. It is a way of putting out the welcome mat and inviting them to share whatever they deem important.

Different communicators have different areas of interest and expertise.

Spirit people who are still identified with their "earth-time personalities" are more likely to want to help with everyday things – finding that perfect dress for a wedding or a new car. A deceased real estate agent may come through to help someone with their housing situation.

Guardian angels are often known to step in to save a person from potential accidents or things like that. There are lots of stories of such things happening. Of course, they also help with finding car keys and parking places, as well as being an endless source of love and embracing help.

There are also those in the *wider reality* who specifically want to teach us about greater truths and understandings. These helpful beings have their agendas, too. They often want to influence us to move forward in our spiritual development as individuals and as a whole (as the human race).

Esther Hicks channels a group of entities that go by the name of Abraham. Their teachings are especially useful for people who want to become more adept at handling their life situations. Abraham explains about manifestation, getting along better with others, and developing people's personal power through gaining control of their thought patterns. In addition to lecturing, Abraham dialogues with individuals in a public forum as a way to instruct the larger group about how they can handle their own life's challenges.

Lee Carroll brings through a being called Kryon who calls himself the Magnetic Master. His primary purpose seems to be to assist the earth as a whole with transitioning into a new era. Kryon gives his viewpoints on current events – such as politics, scientific discoveries, and earth changes – that are happening in the world. He does not dialogue with individuals about their personal situations.

Paul Selig channels a group called "The Guides." Their role here appears to be helping anyone who is ready to lift themselves into what the guides call the "Upper Room." This is a way to describe an individual raising themselves into a Christ-consciousness state. The guides do this through giving instructions of ways for people to attune themselves to that state, especially through declarations. For example, "I know who I am, I know what I am, I know how I serve."

All three of these channelers have been channeling for the spirit world for more than 30 years. They have multiple books and videos that you can watch to learn more about them.

When you make your own connections with members of the *wider reality*, the ones who will be drawn to you will have similar areas of interest to you. I, Ruth, have the "teacher vibration" so the ones in spirit who also teach are the easiest ones for me to connect with. When I was doing the healing work, there were healers in the *wider reality* that worked with me in spirit and instructed me on how to best serve in that capacity.

So whatever your particular interests are, there are also those in the *wider reality* that share those interests, too. They will be the easiest ones for you to connect with because they are ready and eager to interact with you in those areas.

Three Messages for the Readers of This Book

Beloved friends, we are delighted to have this forum to address you once again. We say, "once again," because the dialogue between us is an ongoing one (although the awareness of that may not be in the forefront of your minds).

The comings and goings of spirit in your life is continual. It is more like a slipping in and out of sleep, but in this case a slipping in and out of an awareness of who you truly are.

You may find a sort of resistance come up in you when we introduce to you the idea that many of the thoughts in your own minds are not of your own personal design, for the ease with which communications travel from one to another is far easier than you may imagine.

All of it is truly of a piece. By that we mean that it is all contained in a Unity of What We All Truly Are. That includes you AND every other being in the wider world.

Because that is a lot to "stomach," you are in a habit of seeing just a small portion of What Is. This works well for you – keeping things in bite-sized portions makes it all more palatable.

When you feel a drawing or nudging to expand into new areas that are at present quite foreign to you, we would encourage gathering up both your courage and fortitude and setting out on that blessed journey. For more glory and enchantment will always present itself when you step out of the everyday norms of your present-day life.

There is no urgency or pressure to embark on this journey before the inner desire strikes you, for you do actually have a perfect inner timing "device" that will direct you to look outside at new avenues when the time is right for you.

We celebrate your own departures on such journeys and assure you that along the way there will be multiple opportunities to access any help you may need in the upcoming deliciously exciting situations that you will face.

It is all a glorious journey of the soul of One to all of the rest that belongs there, too. We are all in this together!! Call on any one of us whenever you choose. We love you deeply. More than you might even expect.

****

Two Messages Regarding the Present Time
March 2021

Hold on to your hats, dear friends, the speed and rapid turns in your journeys will continue to increase. Whether you find this to be "good" or not is your own particular preference, but how you view it or hold it within yourself will not change the outcomes of the rapid developments around you.

Take heart, for the courage, strength, and fortitude you may need at times are ever-present within you. And the help you may need at certain points is ever-available to you. You are much stronger and wiser than you think. We love you always.

****

The delight which is potential in this particular era is what one could call a different "flavor" or "vibration." This delight has a resonance/flavor which will feel foreign to you at times and at the same time will feel like an old [comfortable] shoe.

There has been talk about always looking forward [in this coming time], and being open to that which is new and not attached to that which was, and all these sorts of things. But we would also like to point out that as you step more and more into this next phase, that there will indeed be a comfort level which was perhaps unprecedented in your previous activities.

So on the one hand, where it may feel that it is "new" in a sense, there will also be an increase in the comfort that you feel in doing these actions. In other words, as you step into these (what one could call) "newer" endeavors, you will feel more comfortable doing them than perhaps anything else you have done up until this point.

There was a bit of "worry" about the learning curve. We would say that, although there is perhaps a bit of a learning curve, that one might think of it instead as a sinking even more deeply into that which suits you even more perfectly than what you have done up until this point.

For when your true essence is tapped into, there is both a comfort and a power which enables you, therefore, to supersede what has come before and in all directions.

By that, we mean that it supersedes the ability to solve the various challenges that come up. And it supersedes the fulfillment that comes about, and it also supersedes, perhaps even for some of you, the monetary remunerations.

We would say, as you hold it within yourself (as you look towards your future) to perhaps hold it in this context:

> *Rather than a searching in an unknown cavern where it would be difficult to see and hard to know what is next, and such things, we would rather suggest that it is more like when one turns and sees that behind them the sun is rising, and one is flooded with the light and the energy of the divine within self and around self.*

A much different way, perhaps, to view your future.

****

Ecstatic Poetry

As you continue to work with the guides and teachers in spirit and allow yourself to even more easily receive their wisdom and loving influence, you may have the experience of going into an exalted state where you feel carried away in a glorious flow.

The words coming through can begin to have a rhythm and rhyme to them. Do your best to stay with it and allow this gift of spirit to flow through you.

Unfortunately, this tends to happen when we are in the bathtub, dancing on the beach, or engaged in some other activity where paper and pen are nowhere near. If you have something to record with, turn it on!

If you are lucky enough to feel this exalted state coming on while you are writing, do your best to simply record what is coming through you without paying attention to whether it makes sense or rhymes correctly. You can always do some editing afterwards.

There are different parts of the brain that perform different types of tasks. The part of our brains that are active when we are evaluating, judging, or organizing can easily override the part of your mind that is allowing this inspired flow to come about.

Brazilian Trance Mediums

There were some interesting brain studies done on Brazilian Spiritist mediums. The Spiritists (not to be confused with Spiritualists) in Brazil have a vibrant tradition of people going into trance and channeling deceased people through painting, speaking, playing music, and writing (with eyes closed).

The most famous Brazilian trance writer was Francesco (Chico) Xavier. See the movies: *The Mothers of Chico Xavier* and *The Astral City ("Our Home")*.

You can watch some of the trance artists demonstrate on YouTube. Search for "Luiz Gasparetto" and "José Madrado."

The ten mediums in the brain study had been doing the writing in trance for 15-47 years. 2-18 times per month, they channeled letters for people from their deceased friends and relatives.

Note that the Brazilian Spiritists do not take any payments for the channelings they do. They see it as a gift from God that they simply pass on to others. Unlike mediums in the USA who do mediumship as a profession, the Brazilian Spiritists need to hold other jobs.

The brain study showed that while they were writing in trance, the parts of their brains that put words into logical verbal sequences were barely active – a bit like a person who has drunk too much alcohol.

However, the writing they did in that state was more advanced than their normal writing abilities.

When they were in trance, the sentences tended to be longer and the language used was more articulate.

The original study, "Neuroimaging during Trance State: A Contribution to the Study of Dissociation," was published on PLOS_ONE_Group on 21 Nov 2012.

You can also read about this study in two articles that give brief summaries about the experiments – see:

LifeScience.com, "How a Medium's Brain Changes in a Trance State,"

Forbes.com, "When You Inject Spirit Mediums' Brains with Radioactive Chemicals, Strange Things Happen."

****

CHAPTER SEVEN

Gaining Confidence

Skills, Discernment, and Confirmations

Skills

As a professional musician, I had the privilege of performing with some of the most well-known musicians of the day. Some were pop singers who performed shows throughout the world. Each night the songs were performed in the same order with the same introductions and jokes. A core group of backup musicians traveled with them to be sure the accompaniments were consistent. The classical musicians that came to perform concertos with my orchestra, did something similar in that they played the same concerto over and over with different orchestras around the country.

All of that regularity made it possible for these performers to walk out on stage with the confidence that came from thousands of hours of performing the same music. But...

But each night was also different. The orchestras or additional hired-on backup musicians in each city (like myself), were different, each concert hall was a bit different, some days their health was not as good. All those new or different factors were challenges they had to face. But having done a good job of performing so many, many times, gave them a pretty clear idea about what sorts of results to expect.

Confidence is earned. It comes from hours and hours of practice during which a skill is developed bit by bit. There isn't any other way to have the consistency with results. A professional basketball player may have a goal of making 200 successful foul shots a day, just to "keep on his game."

Any action that demands skill, whether it is in sports, music, dance, cooking, plumbing, or even changing a diaper, needs to be done multiple times successfully to gain confidence.

This is also true for gaining confidence with the connections to the *wider reality*. As was stated earlier in this book, TRIAL AND ERROR is the path to developing any skill. So that is also true with this. In the exercises presented here, you commit to a particular answer to a question, and then test it by seeing what the results are. The yes/no questions and the FreeCell game are examples of this.

For developing these skills, the learning curve is shortened *significantly* when you are able to **be aware of your state while making a choice.**

Each state is like a different flavor that becomes something you can recognize. You can look for clues in how you feel in your body as you perceive an answer, as well as how you breathe, how your voice sounds, images that come to you... You eventually learn to recognize when you are "on track" or "in tune," and when you are not.

John Grinder, one of the founders of NLP (neuro-linguistic programming) developed a technique called "modeling." That is a way to speed up developing a skill by sort of "cloning" it from another person. You might find that learning about this technique helps you with increasing the speed that you learn the skills in this book. In this case, you want to "clone" your own behaviors when you are successful, when it works for you.

Being fully aware and *present in the moment while observing yourself* both when it works and when it doesn't (for example with the yes/no exercises) will benefit you tremendously as you solidify your skills.

Intent and Discernment

The *wider reality* is a busy place. If you visited a new country, you would find all sorts of people there. Some of them would be able to speak your language, others would not. Some would have particular skills that would be helpful to you, others not. Some of them would be pleasant, fun, uplifting people you would like to have as friends, and there would be others it would be better to avoid.

"Birds of a feather flock together." That is true to a certain extent here in our physical world, but in the *wider reality*, that is the law of the land. Whether you are aware of it or not, your own beliefs, likes and dislikes – the lens through which you see the world – is like a welcoming doorway for those you have contact with in the *wider reality*.

This is why **intent** is so important.

If your intent is to grow and become more able to benefit others, you will be dialing up those in the *wider reality* who also desire to benefit others. It is like joining the club of those who serve the Whole.

If your intent is to fully develop your creative or inventive gifts (which in turn will expand the world) there will be those in the *wider reality* who also have this desire for you. They will step forward to assist in any endeavor that will increase your abilities to use those special gifts.

It is therefore important when asking for help to be clear about what we want and who we are open to interacting with. As previously stated, I choose only to interact with those who are loving, wise, and helpful, ALL THREE. No one else is welcome at my *wider reality* table.

Monroe Institute, "Guidelines"

As I explored some of the environments in the *wider reality* during a weeklong training (*Guidelines*) at the Monroe Institute in Virginia, there were multiple "beings" that presented themselves to me. The first one started off interacting with me in a way that seemed helpful, but as it continued, I noticed there was a certain vibe. His statements seemed designed to pump up my ego. That was a definite red flag.

Remember that the place of truth is the place to be. If something veers off of that, it is only one thing, *off course.*

Whether it is pumping our egos up or knocking them down, the result is the same. Anything like that is a hook to create a need. In this case, it would be a need to continue feeling a pumped-up ego. That could easily flip to going the other way – insults also activate our egos because we want to correct the situation and get back to feeling good again. So, a need gets created either way – being knocked down or boosted up.

I had been on the spiritual path long enough to pick up on the ego-stroking manipulation, so I rejected this one. "Not interested. Leave." He simply disappeared because he had to leave when I switched myself off from being in sync with him.

Two more less-than-worthwhile beings presented themselves and were also rejected. Then the "big guys" came in. The love that came with them was so wonderful and clear. The first thing they communicated was, "Good job. We would not have been able to be here with you if you had settled for less." Wow.

If you are unsure about some "being" you become aware of, you can always say, "Let me feel your love" or some other little test that you devise that feels good to you – something that aligns with your own views about what is good and right.

Anything that feels hurtful, creepy, or unpleasant is not anything you need to engage with. There is absolutely no reason for you to participate with anything unpleasant. There are shamans that have as their service to help and heal those who need it in the *wider reality*, but this is not something to step into on your own.

Wise and Loving Help

The *wider-reality* guides and teachers can be a great help with our ongoing personal development. We all have our own issues to work on and deal with. Focusing on improving those is both a gift to ourselves and to everyone else we have contact with.

The beautiful loving ones I interact with in the *wider reality* repeatedly impress me with their ability to see each of us through the eyes of love. They operate in truth and are not swayed by the opinions of the ego-self in the way that we often are. They are my heroes!

Suggestions vs Commands

One way to distinguish the loving, wise ones is that they never tell us what we *ought* to do, and they certainly never threaten us in any way. They make suggestions only. It can even be a bit amusing how they will express such things. Instead of saying, "What?! Are you kidding? That would be a stupid thing to do!!" they are more likely to say something like, "If you choose to do that, there could be some difficulties that will come along as a result. However, if you instead do xyz, we believe you will be more pleased with that result."

Your Own Inner Knowing/Intuition

If, instead of dialoging with someone in the *wider reality*, you are tuning into your own inner knowing/intuition, you can, of course, get helpful answers that way, too. When it comes to everyday choices, this is probably what you are more likely to do. Either way, we can get good help with the choices where the answers are not obvious to us right away!

Getting Confirmations from Other Sources

One more concept to include here is that you can also ask for confirmations on anything you feel is being communicated to you from the *wider reality*. It is completely okay to say to the spirit world that you would like an additional sign to help you with any doubt you may have about what is coming through to you. There is no judgment of you for asking such a thing.

Your unquestioning faith is not expected or even encouraged. Being told not to question, is a definite red flag that there is untruth going on. The truth can withstand any test you make of it. Like testing a floorboard to see if it will hold up under pressure, anything you are going to rely on should be able to withstand your tests.

Example: *Helen is considering quitting her job. She believes that the guidance she received from her inspired writing is encouraging her to make the change. But this is a big choice. She wants to be really certain that leaving the job is the best thing to do right now. In her own way, she makes a prayer in the morning and says, "I need a sign. Please help."*

#1. As she is driving to work, she sees a billboard that says, "What's new is always better!" Hmmm... Could that be a sign? She isn't sure. When she gets to work, there is a weird sort of vibe in the office. She feels like people are looking away and pretending not to notice her. She goes to check her mail and there is a pink slip there. She has been fired.

Well, that certainly makes it easier. Now she can collect unemployment while she looks for a better job.

#2. As Helen is driving to work, she stops at a light behind a car with a window sticker that says, "Salve Regina University." Her first thought is how lucky they must be. Salve Regina has a wonderful Expressive Arts program. Helen wishes she could do something like that. The song that comes on the radio is singing, "You are more than this."

When she gets to work and opens her email, she sees an ad that pops up about Salve Regina University (!). She probably shouldn't be doing that now, but she clicks on the link and it tells about scholarships that are being offered. She sends the link to her private email to look at later.

At the lunch restaurant, the tables are all taken and she is about to eat her sandwich standing up when a woman sitting alone indicates that it is okay to share her table. Helen is grateful. Strangely enough, the woman has a briefcase with the Salve Regina logo on it. Helen plucks up her courage and asks the woman about the university.

Fast forward... not only does Helen quit her job, but she also begins a program at Salve Regina that fulfills her deepest desires of what to do in her life.

#3. *Helen loves the Runes, the I Ching, and also the Tarot Cards. She consults all of them about the job situation. Interestingly enough, they all are giving similar messages to leave the job, even though they have very different ways of saying it.*

Confirmation Signs You See by Chance

The ways that we each feel good about receiving the additional confirmations are very broad. Below are some possibilities that can get you thinking about what you may want to have your eye out for (if you ask for additional confirmations).

Also see *Highlighting* and *Body Pointing* (page 27-28). The strongest indicators are ones that are a bit surprising or that show up in a place you would not expect.

- words or phrases on bumper stickers, billboards or trucks
- book titles or a sentence in a book feels like it is highlighted
- pictures that remind you of things or are symbolic
- posts and ads online
- rainbows, sundogs, claps of thunder, a ray of sun on just one thing, Jacob's ladders (sun through clouds)
- cloud patterns or shapes
- beach stones – shapes, associations
- birds that have meaning to you, or other animals that you have memories or associations with that are meaningful
- feathers, butterflies
- numbers that have meaning, birthdays, wedding dates, repeating numbers – 1111, 333...
- songs – for the lyrics and/or associations and memories
- letters in the mail
- coins, especially pennies, found money, unexpected money
- people make statements or tell you a story
- smells that have a meaning to you
- electric lights flashing or turning on or off

- body sensations – tingles, chills, churning stomach, involuntary laughter or smiling
- vivid dreams can serve as a confirmation or warning about a choice we are contemplating

Other Sources of Guidance

Whether it was throwing bones or dice, reading tea leaves, or using a flat surface for scrying, people have been using different divination tools for as long as we know. You may like to use one of these as an additional way to check on the answers you get through your intuitive inner knowing and the inspired writing.

This is different than simply being on the lookout for any spontaneous signs you notice. The Tarot, I Ching, and Runes are common tools for gleaning guidance about life's situations.

Recognizing a Presence

As you continue doing the connecting with the helpful ones in the *wider reality*, you may become attuned to feeling their presence around you even when you are not doing the writing. Here are a few things to be on the lookout for. These things could indicate a spirit guide or spirit person is with you. It can also be that someone here is thinking of you.

What makes these things notable – worth paying attention to – is that they aren't related to something you were already thinking about. They pop in out of nowhere (see page 28, *Hits and Nudges*).

- Faces of people appear in your mind.
  This could mean that someone is thinking of you.

- Memories, ideas, or songs pop into your mind.
  These can function as a sort of calling card from people in
  spirit who want to connect with you or send you their love
  and greetings.

- A feeling like the person is there with you.
  Like the pets mentioned earlier, the person in spirit may be
  stopping in for a visit. Greet them with the bond of love that
  you two share.

- Hearing their voice in your head.
  They are literally speaking to you. Listen up!

There are many more ways that those in the spirit world will let
you know they are present. See the examples on pages 116-
117 for more ideas about how they make themselves known to
you.

An Opportunity We All Share

Becoming more in tune with our own inner knowing and
accessing the help available to us in the *wider reality* makes
such a big difference. When we feel clear and sure of the
choices we are making, life gets a lot easier.

I hope that this book has given you lots of opportunities and
encouragement to pursue your ability to tap into the vast pool
of help that is right here, right now, for each one of us.

To all those who have ears, let them hear!

****

About the Author

Like many entrepreneurs, Ruth Shilling, M.M., has had a many-faceted career. Throughout all her endeavors, she has had a keen interest in personal empowerment and spiritual development. She began as a professional musician and teacher, has authored a number of books on different topics, taught various healing modalities and empowerment strategies at centers throughout the USA and Canada, and has founded an Egypt tour company.

As a musician, she began with five years studying classical music (viola) in Germany where she played in a number of orchestras and ensembles. After receiving her Masters in Music Performance, she taught violin, viola, chamber music, and String Methods at the University of Connecticut. She was also the principal viola of the New London, CT, ECSO for 17 years, performed with a number of other professional groups, and made some recordings.

As the owner and operator of the *All One World Egypt Tours* business, Ruth has traveled to Egypt 50+ times over the last 25 years.

Through her publishing company, *All One World Books & Media,* she now publishes books by other authors as well as her own books about personal empowerment, musical performance, and Egyptian subjects. See those listed on the next page.

ruthshilling.com

Books and Cards by Ruth Shilling

Through A Medium's Eyes Series: About Life, Love, Mediumship, and the Spirit World

- Rev. B. Anne Gehman, Volume 1 (also in LARGE PRINT)
- Carol Gasber, Volume 2
- Neal Rzepkowski, M.D., Volume 3

EGYPT

Ancient Egyptian Gods & Goddess CARDS

The Tomb of Queen Nefertari: Egyptian Gods and Goddesses of the New Kingdom

Time & Space in the Temples & Pyramids: All One World Egypt Tour

SINAI: The Desert & Bedouins of South Sinai's Central Regions (photo book with text)

Violin Success Series

- Success with the Violin & Life: Strategies, Techniques, and Tips for Learning Quickly and Doing Well, Volume 1

- Performing at Your Best: A Musician's Guide to Successful Performances, Volume 2

"Color It True" Manifestation Mandalas Coloring Book Series

- Marvelous Manifestation Mandalas, Volume 1
- Magnetic Manifestation Mandalas, Volume 2
- Miraculous Manifestation Mandalas, Volume 3
- Angelic Manifestation Mandalas, Volume 4

Where to Find Ruth Shilling

Blogs, Interviews, Videos, and More

Webs: ruthshilling.com, all1world.com

Blogs: LovingWiseOnes.wordpress.com, FlowOfWellBeing.wordpress.com

Interviews: ruthshilling.com/interviews

Private Sessions: spiritualmedium1.com

Egypt Tours: timespace-egypttour.com, 1worldtours.com

Facebook: facebook.com/ruthshillingmm

****

Made in the USA
Middletown, DE
23 May 2021